At David C Cook, we equip the local church around the corner and around the globe to make disciples. Come see how we are working together—go to **www.davidccook.org**. Thank you!

DAVID C COOK

transforming lives together

What people are saying about …

CALMING ANGRY KIDS

"I was immediately drawn to *Calming Angry Kids* because my family has had some high emotions over the years. As I read Tricia Goyer's book, I felt encouragement and not shame. I felt as though Tricia was sitting next to me sharing her personal stories and giving me help, guidance, and encouragement for my own parenting journey. If you have a child who struggles with anger, sit with Tricia and let her encourage you as well."

—**Jamie Ivey**, bestselling author of
If You Only Knew, host of the podcast
The Happy Hour with Jamie Ivey

"From the very first words of *Calming Angry Kids*, my heart resonated with Tricia's story. Loving children from hard places is a beautiful calling and one that is very lonely at times. Tricia offers insight and wisdom for parents struggling with anger in their homes. She makes you feel as if she is in your corner, fighting with you for the heart of your child."

—**Natalie Gwyn**, speaker,
author of *Okayest Mom*

"As a mom of angry kids (who also struggles with anger myself!), I need this book. Tricia has faithfully hiked this rocky path of calming angry kids, and I am selfishly very grateful she has put her experiences into a handbook for the rest of us. This will be my go-to resource for years to come."

—**Emily Thomas**, host of *The Mom Struggling Well* podcast

"These words from Tricia are whispers of hope. They offer a healing way forward for those who have felt stuck. Read them and sigh with gratitude and relief, like I did."

—**Sara Hagerty**, author of *Every Bitter Thing Is Sweet* and *Unseen: The Gift of Being Hidden in a World that Loves to be Noticed*

"Oh, weary parent, you know the pain, guilt, and challenge of parenting an angry child. In these pages you'll find hope, because author Tricia Goyer understands the struggle. With a mix of journal-level authenticity and practical guide, you'll find a trusted friend to help identify your own emotions and lead your child to a calmer place."

—**Heather MacFadyen**, host of *God Centered Mom* podcast

"A gold mine for the weary! This book is packed with game-changing tools and soul-soothing wisdom."

—**Patricia Beal**, author of *A Season to Dance* and mama in the whirlwind

"Peace is contagious, and we desperately need it to consume our homes. Tricia provides the help overwhelmed parents need to not only calm their kids but also themselves in the process. Grace flows through these pages to move from anger to a place of love, joy, peace, and self-control."

—**Dr. Saundra Dalton-Smith**, physician,
author of *Sacred Rest: Recover Your Life,*
Renew Your Energy, Restore Your Sanity

"I have worked closely with Tricia Goyer and witnessed her ability to skillfully integrate her parenting experience, her work with clinical professionals, and her faith to better understand and effectively improve her relationships with her own children. I am grateful and encouraged that Tricia has made the extraordinary effort to share her hard-earned knowledge and experience. She truly recognizes the importance of fostering self-regulation and attachment in parent-child relationships, and provides useful, supportive strategies and resources for struggling caregivers. I recommend *Calming Angry Kids* to those who face the challenging and rewarding work of helping traumatized and angry children heal."

—**Ashley Huddleston**, LCSW,
child and family therapist

"Tricia Goyer truly gets it! She has a deep understanding of how angry children impact the family. Her nonjudgmental and humorous approach to the subject offers parents practical guidance to help both the child and the family heal. I recommend this book not only to parents who live in the chaos of children who rage, but to all parents as a guide book for practicing patience and loving on those kids who need it the most."

—**Dr. Martha Wall-Whitfield**, principal at
Arkansas Juvenile Assessment and Treatment
Center, gang specialist, foster/adoptive parent

"Tricia Goyer is a passionate advocate for kids from hard places and offers hope and healing to the parents who love them every day."

—**Jason Weber**, National Director of Foster
Care Initiatives, Christian Alliance for Orphans

"Like sitting down to chat with a good friend, this conversational book shares personal experiences from Tricia Goyer's precious family along with advice from professionals to equip families in diffusing their children's anger and moving to healthy communication. A practical and necessary handbook for all parent parents and a must-read for foster and adoptive families, with practical tools and strategies to help their children heal from past trauma."

—**Julia DesCarpentrie**, adoption and foster care
advocate, county cordinator with The CALL

"I've personally witnessed the beautiful transformation of the Goyer family as Tricia and John have patiently walked through many ups and downs to find their family's new and inspiring normal. Without sugarcoating, Tricia invites parents in the whirlwind like herself to stick with their kids no matter what. Full of tools and suggestions,

Tricia offers much-needed advice and encouragement to those who want to provide a home and family that's full of hope and healing."

—**Eric Gilmore**, MSW, founding
director of Immerse Arkansas

"What a Godsend! Reading *Calming Angry Kids* is like having a heart-to-heart over coffee with someone who gets it. A must-read for all parents and anyone who cares for kids from hard places."

—**Alison Bryant**, MA, LBSW,
social worker, adoptive parent

"Tricia Goyer has done an amazing job of providing practical solutions and equipping parents to calm angry children and manage their own angry responses. The chapter included for families involved in foster care, adoption, and childhood trauma is especially helpful as these situations call for additional, intentional bonding and interventions. The 'Scriptures for Families to Memorize' in the back is a bonus we will use often in our counseling practices. I highly recommend *Calming Angry Kids* to families with children of all ages."

—**Michelle Nietert**, MA, LPC-S, clinical
director of Community Counseling Associates

CALMING
ANGRY
KIDS

help and hope for parents in the whirlwind

tricia goyer

DAVID C COOK

transforming lives together

CALMING ANGRY KIDS
Published by David C Cook
4050 Lee Vance Drive
Colorado Springs, CO 80918 U.S.A.

Integrity Music Limited, a Division of David C Cook
Eastbourne, East Sussex BN23 6NT, England

The graphic circle C logo is a registered trademark of David C Cook.

The website addresses recommended throughout this book are offered as a
resource to you. These websites are not intended in any way to be or imply an
endorsement on the part of David C Cook, nor do we vouch for their content.

Details in some stories have been changed to protect the privacy of the persons involved.

This book details the author's personal experiences with and opinions about parenting
angry children. The author is not licensed as an educational consultant, teacher,
psychologist, or psychiatrist. This book is meant only to help and guide you; it is not
meant to be used, nor should it be used, to diagnose or treat any medical or psychological
condition. If your child is doing any of the following, seek immediate help from a
professional: (1) hurting self, (2) hurting others, or (3) destroying property.

Unless otherwise noted, all Scripture quotations are taken from THE HOLY BIBLE, NEW
INTERNATIONAL VERSION®, NIV® Copyright © 1973, 1978, 1984, 2011 by Biblica,
Inc.® Used by permission. All rights reserved worldwide. Scripture quotations marked ESV
are taken from the ESV® Bible (The Holy Bible, English Standard Version®), copyright ©
2001 by Crossway, a publishing ministry of Good News Publishers. Used by permission. All
rights reserved; THE MESSAGE are taken from THE MESSAGE. Copyright © by Eugene
H. Peterson 1993, 2002. Used by permission of Tyndale House Publishers, Inc.; NASB are
taken from the New American Standard Bible®, copyright © 1960, 1995 by The Lockman
Foundation. Used by permission. (www.Lockman.org); NLT are taken from the *Holy Bible*,
New Living Translation, copyright © 1996, 2007 by Tyndale House Foundation. Used by
permission of Tyndale House Publishers, Inc., Carol Stream, Illinois 60188. All rights reserved.

LCCN 2018937287
ISBN 978-1-4347-1100-7
eISBN 978-0-8307-7572-9

© 2018 Tricia Goyer
Published in association with the literary agency of Books & Such Literary Management,
52 Mission Circle, Suite 122, PMB 170, Santa Rosa, CA 95409-5370, www.booksandsuch.com.

The Team: Alice Crider, Liz Heaney, Rachael Stevenson, Diane Gardner, Susan Murdock
Cover Design: Ashley Ward
Cover Image: Getty Images

Printed in the United States of America
First Edition 2018

4 5 6 7 8 9 10 11 12 1

021819

To my children, true gifts from God.
And to John, my gentle warrior. I'm thankful I'm
walking this parenting path with you by my side.

CONTENTS

Acknowledgments   17

Introduction: A Heartbreakingly Angry Home   19

Part 1: Understanding Anger: Theirs and Yours

1. Trauma and the Truth behind Mad   29

2. Anger from Life Stressors   41

3. Physical Issues That Can Fuel Anger   51

4. A Parent,s Internal Response to Anger   67

5. A Parent,s External Response to Anger   81

Part 2: Helping Your Angry Kid

6. Building Bonds   97

7. Stopping the Cycle before It Starts   111

8. Teaching Kids to Calm Themselves   131

9. Calming Angry Babies, Toddlers, and Preschoolers   149

10. Calming Preteen Anger   167

11. Calming Teen Anger   179

12. A Healing Place for Adopted and Foster Kids   195

Conclusion: The Victor,s Crown   213

Appendix A. Scriptures to Memorize as a Family   217

Appendix B. Recommended Resources   221

Notes   229

ACKNOWLEDGMENTS

Recently my kids and I were talking about the release of *Calming Angry Kids*.

"You can thank us now," my daughter Grace said with a smirk.

"Excuse me?"

"Well, if it wasn't for us being so angry you wouldn't have been able to write about angry kids."

I chuckled about that, and deep down I know she's right. Having angry kids was hard, but I do have a lot of things to be thankful for. Learning to calm angry kids has drawn me closer to God, my husband, therapists, and friends who have been there to support me. I've been stretched, and I've found ways to bring help and hope to others, so I suppose I should acknowledge my kids … uh, thank you. But I will say that I'm also thankful most of these angry issues are in the past.

I'm thankful my husband John has been there for late-night chats as we've working through these issues and tried to figure out how to help our kids. I'm thankful for my adult kids Cory, Leslie, and Nathan who've been completely supportive during this journey. I'm thankful for dear friends who were available to pray for me night and day: Rebecca, Amber, Tracy, Pam, Cara, and Terri Lyn.

Thank you for being available and sending prayers of comfort when I needed them most.

Thank you to the wonderful team of therapists and All Children's Academy and The Child Study Center who helped (and are still helping) to guide my kids along their healing journey.

Finally, I'm thankful for my agent Janet Grant, my editor Alice Crider, and the amazing team at David C Cook who made this book possible.

And Jesus, I couldn't have walked this journey without you. Thank you.

A HEARTBREAKINGLY ANGRY HOME

My heart pounded as I mounted the stairs, the screams of four teen girls striking my ears. "Hurry! Maddie's climbing out the window!" my fifteen-year-old daughter Anna called.

"John!" I yelled down the stairs as I quickened my steps. "I need your help!"

Though nearly bedtime, no one would be going to bed anytime soon. The conflict had started between two of the teens during dinner. Maddie, the aggressor this time, and Grace, the victim.

I stepped between them before they came to blows and attempted to calm their anger. Yet when I tried to speak some reason and defend Grace, who was receiving the brunt of her sister's anger that night, Grace turned on me and jumped to her sister's side.

Seriously? I try to help you, and now I'm the bad guy?

Soon a third sister joined her siblings against me, each upset—unified in their anger.

My head throbbed. My heart ached.

For the previous six years everything in these girls' lives had been an uphill battle. In foster care, the four sisters had lived apart as often as they'd lived together. Supposedly trustworthy adults had promised to care for them and never leave them yet had tossed them to the curb again and again when the girls' anger became too much to handle.

But knowing my daughters' traumatic history didn't ease the pain of the moment. *I don't want to deal with their fighting again … I can't handle this … What did we get ourselves into?*

As I stood in the bedroom, the three sisters still raged, and the fourth, Anna, began shouting at them: "You're going to ruin this. You're going to ruin this!"

Tears ran down Anna's cheeks and fear filled her eyes. *Please don't send us away,* she pleaded silently. As the oldest, she knew what would keep the sisters together: compliance and obedience—something her siblings couldn't manage.

The four sisters had been removed from their biological parents and then placed in one foster home after another, finally ending up in a children's home. Then came the failed adoption. They transferred out of that home just eleven months before moving into ours. Their hurt remained an open wound.

Then they were brought to John and me—two overly optimistic parents who'd dared to welcome four more children into our home shortly after adopting three other children, including two preschoolers considered special needs for behavior issues.

With a trembling sigh, I patted Anna's shoulder and told her I'd take over. I surveyed the girls' bedroom. The window was indeed open. Screen mangled. Curtain rod broken. Curtain twisted. Fear upped the anger-induced adrenaline that already pumped through me. The driveway was a second-story drop below. Did Maddie really think she could climb down the rain gutter and survive?

My teeth clenched. My hands balled at my side. "What do you think you're doing?"

"I wasn't really going to climb out. I don't want to die!" Maddie shouted back. She rolled her eyes at me like I was stupid.

"Then why is the window open? Do you want to break your neck?" Cold air from outside raised goose bumps on my arms—or were they from the image that filled my mind of her broken body sprawled on the cement below?

Maddie rushed to the closet, pulled items off hangers, and shoved them into a duffel bag.

"What do you think you're doing?"

"Leaving."

My voice rose again. "And do you think that's going to solve anything?"

She didn't respond. Instead, she threw her duffel bag into the hall. Without thinking, I followed her into the hall. But when Maddie turned and stomped back into her room, I grabbed her duffel and rushed to my bedroom. Then I hurled the bag into my closet, hiding it. I did the same with the other two duffels she had packed earlier. A few minutes later, the discovery that her bags were missing fueled her fire, but I knew she wouldn't run without them.

By the time I'd hidden the duffels, John had taken over. The gentle dad, he was able to calm the girls and talk some sense into them. It would take some time, but I hoped by lights-out the sisters would be reconciled. As for how they would treat me, it all depended. Usually after this type of blow-up, when I tried to calm their anger, I'd be labeled the bad guy. That meant days of getting the cold shoulder. Often I'd hear the girls talking but they'd stop as I entered the room. I never knew the silent treatment could hurt so much, especially when I was just trying to love them, give them a home, and be their mom.

I shuffled into the younger kids' room with weary steps. Sniffling sounds came from their three beds.

"Why do they act so mean?" Sissy asked.

"Did she climb out the window?" Aly wanted to know.

The youngest, Buddy, just sat in his bed and rubbed his eyes.

"They're still learning how to deal with their anger. Daddy and I tried to help them," I explained. "Why don't we pray for your sisters … pray for all of us?"

Yet even as the kids prayed, worried thoughts filled my mind. *This isn't right. This isn't fair to the little kids. What type of home has this turned into?* Our once-peaceful home had become an angry home. A heartbreakingly angry home.

Dozens of times a day these questions replayed in my mind: *How can I help my kids? What can we do to find calm?*

Hope for Angry Kids

If you've picked up this book, it's for a reason. Maybe, like me, you have a heartbreakingly angry home. Or a heartbreakingly angry kid who doesn't lash out in the ways I describe but who is slowly pulling inward, drawn into an emotional black hole by anger shoved deep inside. Maybe, like ours, your angry kids are adopted. Or maybe not. Angry kids grow up in all types of homes. Sometimes it is not external situations that cause kids to be so angry but rather internal ones.

You most likely never pictured yourself in this situation. As a ten-year-old, when you imagined yourself as a parent, you likely didn't think about calming kids after rages or trying to hide your tears as your child throws a tantrum in the middle of the cereal aisle at the grocery store. But in the hard way life works, trying to calm angry kids—while still keeping your own sanity and peaceful heart—defines your life. You don't just have a kid who gets frustrated and angry from time to time; you have an angry kid.

What is an "angry kid"? A child known for episodes of anger—meltdowns and aggression—multiple times a week (although he may be silent and sullen). Angry kids have trouble handling their emotions and frequently direct their anger at their caregivers. They often feel sorry for their actions after they've worn themselves out and calmed down, but that doesn't erase what happened.

If you are parenting an angry child, you'd give anything for tools and ideas to help your child. Yet where do you find them? It's not as if every parent in your cul-de-sac faces these same issues. Sometimes you feel isolated and alone.

That's one reason I wrote this book—so you won't feel alone. Or frustrated. Or hopeless. I'm writing to you as a mom who's experienced all these feelings. There were days I couldn't think of one person I could reach out to for advice—someone who understood. Some days I questioned whether anything would change, and I feared that the future would just get worse not better. Some days I wanted to lock my bedroom door, curl up on my floor, and hide. (Okay, the truth is that really happened.) Most days I'd give anything—anything—for one day of calm.

Many positive things have happened in my home between those angry, drama-filled days and now. We're a new family. Not a perfect family, but one that is mostly peaceful. Of all the things I may have achieved in life, learning to calm angry kids is truly my biggest achievement.

These days I smile when Maddie plops down next to me on the couch, kisses my cheek, and laughs. "Remember that day you hid all my stuff when I tried to run away?"

I laugh with her but with a twinge of ache. Because I know that for every Maddie there's another child out there dealing with anger. And that for every angry child there's a parent who's longing for calm.

Ready to Love and Be Loved

I am not a doctor, psychologist, or therapist. I'm a mom who has spent countless hours in therapy offices because my kids needed help—and I did too. In this book I've gathered some of the best techniques and insights I've learned and expounded on them with the hope of helping you.

I'm also a Christian, and I know my role as a parent is not simply to help my children succeed on earth but also to disciple them so they will be prepared for eternity. When you think about it, everything comes down to our children's hearts—how they interact with the world and how they interact with God. After all, if I can't help my child love, respect, obey, and cherish a relationship with a parent or sibling here on earth, how will he ever open himself up to an unseen God in heaven?

From the moment John and I told our kids we were going to be their forever parents, we chose to stick it out. We were committed to loving these kids, even when they raged, even when it didn't seem like we were getting through. Very quickly we realized that their trauma was causing us trauma, so we sought answers. We had to learn what to do in order to survive. In the process, we not only learned to survive; we learned to thrive. Yes, it is possible, I promise!

As James 1:5 says, "If you need wisdom, ask our generous God, and he will give it to you. He will not rebuke you for asking" (NLT). I'm so thankful God provided me with the wisdom I needed, and that's what I offer you in this book. *Calming Angry Kids* focuses on how you can calm—not ignore, discipline, or demand obedience from—angry children. Angry kids need to be taught how to deal with their anger. And it makes sense. We teach our kids how to do many things—make their beds, brush their teeth, make a sandwich—but we don't often teach them how to deal with their emotions or handle the pain they feel deep inside. But if we are going to help our kids calm themselves, we need to realize that self-regulation—the ability to manage our own emotions and resist impulsive behaviors—isn't just about training; it involves developmental aspects too. No matter their ages, angry children lack the tools, language, impulse control, and problem-solving to do a better job expressing their feelings. And that's this book's purpose—to give you tools to teach your child (and yourself!) how to handle anger—and even prevent anger—in effective ways.

I pray that after reading this book, you will have a sense of peace, knowing it is possible to move your kids away from anger, toward joy and calm. Even more importantly, I pray you'll grow closer to your children as the walls of pain and protection crumble, revealing hearts ready to love and be loved by you and, most of all, by God.

Part 1

UNDERSTANDING ANGER: THEIRS AND YOURS

1

TRAUMA AND THE TRUTH BEHIND MAD

Aly, the first of our adopted children, joined our family as a new-born, and the sibling closest to her age was sixteen years old. So when we told her that we were going to adopt two children who were near her age, three-year-old Aly was excited. Yet we soon real-ized that we had to stay near and keep a close eye as the three of them played together. Both two-year-old Buddy and five-year-old Sissy were easily upset.

Not too many days after Sissy and Buddy moved in, the three children were playing in their bedroom as I folded laundry just out-side the bedroom door. John stood in the hall next to me.

"That's mine!" we heard Aly's small voice cry out.

"No, mine!" Sissy responded.

John quickly stepped into the room and paused. I heard shock in his voice. "Did you just hit your sister?"

The cry that followed pierced the air. It wasn't Aly, the child who'd been hit. (The hit wasn't hard enough for that.) Instead, it was

Sissy. She screamed and threw herself on the floor with a rage we'd never seen in a child before.

I hurried into the bedroom, unsure what had happened. John knelt beside her and attempted to calm her with his words. Her face flamed red, and pure anger flashed in her eyes. She kicked and swung her arms as the two toddlers hurried away from her.

To protect her and the other children, John scooped up Sissy. He cradled her like a baby, but that just angered her more. He sat on the bed and held her tight. "That's okay. It's going to be all right. You're going to be all right."

After that first tantrum, Sissy experienced tantrums on a daily basis. She kicked, screamed, and hit, and she was strong. When John was home, he held her, attempting to protect her and the other kids. When he wasn't home, it was up to me.

In her angry state, Sissy posed a danger to herself and others. Yet when I held her, it seemed to fuel her fury. With all my strength, I'd cradle her in front of me, cuddled up like a mother holding her infant. This allowed me to hold her fists and control her legs—dangling to the side—so she couldn't kick me (which she continually tried to do). In this hold, her face tensed and reddened as she squeezed her eyes shut. Sometimes she screamed mean words and threats. Since she couldn't hurt me with her body, she tried to do it with her words. The last thing she wanted was to make eye contact with me.

But when I looked into my daughter's angry eyes, all I saw was a broken little girl.

"It's okay, Sissy. Everything's going to be okay. I love you. God loves you," I'd speak into her screams. Then I'd pray over her. As her screams quieted, I'd sing Sunday school songs from my childhood. While these things didn't always calm Sissy, they helped calm me.

At first, during these episodes, Sissy jerked and twisted her head, trying to look away. When she did return my gaze, she glared at me with daggers in her eyes. Eventually—after weeks of my holding and cradling her—she started to make eye contact. Even though she struggled and fought, physically demanding I let her go, her eyes said something different. They seemed to plead, *Hold on. Keep clinging to me. Keep fighting for me. Don't let go.*

When John and I first considered adopting kids from foster care, we worried about all the paperwork and home visits that go along with adoption. We were concerned about the expenses, where we'd fit more kids into our lives, and how to prepare our other children for their new siblings. I fretted about new personalities and adding more work to my busy life. I had no idea what would really consume our days: dealing with my children's anger. Buddy made huge messes and destroyed things. Sissy's anger proved all-consuming. By the time they moved in with us, these two young children had stayed in twelve different homes. With a broken heart, I remember one of the first things Sissy ever told me: "I don't like waking up in a new place."

The Truth behind Mad

Can you imagine being a tiny, frail five-year-old shuffled from home to home and expected to trust adults you don't know? Sissy had no place to call her own. She had no control. She had no voice …

except one she used to scream and shout really, really loudly. Anger provided her a way to communicate that things were not right in her world and in her heart.

These kids were strangers to me, just as I was to them. We had no bond. I had not held them as little babies and hugged and kissed them. And even during peaceful moments, they didn't let me get too close or offer much affection.

I wish I could say I was always calm and loving when dealing with my daughter's angry episodes. That's not the case. *I* was angry. I was mad not just because of her actions but also because I couldn't get any work done. Nor could I care for the other kids. While I dealt with Sissy, Buddy and Aly were often fighting each other or getting into stuff. There is no more helpless feeling than holding a raging five-year-old while two toddlers dump boxes of cereal and crackers in the pantry.

But anger wasn't my only negative emotion. I also felt guilt for how adding these two kids was affecting the rest of our family, particularly our teenage son and my grandmother, who lived with us. The peace that once reigned in our home was gone … as was the peace within my own heart.

The truth behind mad is that no one likes it, especially the angry child.

It's not as if Sissy was happy with or thrived on being angry. She seemed to hate it as much as we did. She just didn't know how to handle things differently. She didn't know how to communicate her pain or other emotions. She didn't know how to protect her heart from being hurt again—from being abandoned again—except to act out.

Later, when Sissy and Buddy went to therapy, I learned about the walls they'd erected around their hearts. It was less risky for them to act out than to lower their guard only to be hurt again. It was more empowering for them to be mad than to be sad. It was especially easier to be mad than to be vulnerable and feel powerless. It's amazing how kids push us away, when they really want us to hold them close.

Fight, Flight, or Freeze

Many people think painful things just bounce off kids. They believe children get over such things quickly, but I disagree. Consider your own childhood. What affected you as a child—a loss, a divorce, bullying, neglect? Do you recall angry words that were targeted at you? Has it been easy to get over such things? Have you seen how those painful times affected the rest of your life in big and small ways?

Angry kids do not "just get over" the anger that often accompanies childhood hurts. It will pop up in unexpected ways and in unexpected places, which is why it's vital for us to help our kids now, while they are still young. Anger comes out in small ways when they are little, and it comes out in bigger ways as they grow.

Help is available for angry kids, but first it's important to figure out the underlying causes of our children's anger so we find ways to help calm and heal them. In our family's case, the most obvious cause of our kids' anger was the trauma they had experienced—the neglect in their early childhood and the confusion and pain of being in state care and moved around a lot.

Trauma-triggered anger usually manifests itself in one of three ways: fight, flight, or freeze. But this doesn't apply just to kids who've faced trauma. All children exhibit the same type of responses; actually, we are all wired to protect ourselves. When we sense danger, we will instinctively react with a fight, flight, or freeze response. Not a lot of thought goes into this response. The body just naturally does its thing.

Fight is exhibiting anger in response to pain or danger. It can look like kicking, screaming, gasping for breath, clenching fists, or throwing objects.

Flight is attempting to run away from anything that is causing pain, anger, or other overwhelming emotions. It might include darting eyes, fidgeting, jumping up on a table, or actually running away, often without concern for safety.

Freeze is harder to understand but may involve shutting down, holding one's breath, feeling unable to move, or escaping into one's own mind. When kids "freeze," they are physically present with us but are someplace else mentally. They shut down.

Children respond with fight, flight, or freeze when they feel threatened (even if the danger is only perceived and not an actual danger). Often we parents don't understand what is happening. But what we view as a small problem or unexpected disruption our kids may see as a huge threat. That's because their reaction is not always a response to something happening in that moment. A child's response—including extreme anger—is often tied to something that occurred in her past. Something happening in the present triggered the memory (often unconscious) of what occurred previously.

As a means of protection, a child's subconscious perceives the threat from the past as something threatening her in the present.

For example, a child may feel threatened when seeing a playground swing after she had a bad fall or when recognizing anger on an adult's face, because in the past adult anger led to abuse. Just about anything can seem threatening to a child if trauma is attached to it.

I didn't realize this for many years. I'd express frustration over a messy living room and my child would respond by arguing and fighting with me. Asking her to pick up her socks would lead to a large blowup. Why? The frustrated look in my eyes triggered her "fight" response. Because in her past, situations had escalated quickly—from frustration, to anger, and sometimes to violence—her body learned to prepare for the fight to come.

Things related to the senses—a touch, sound, word or phrase, taste, or smell—also sometimes trigger fight, flight, or freeze responses. Your child may appear to be overreacting, but the reaction actually points to something deeper, something not always connected with past trauma. Even how kids perceive a nonthreatening situation can trigger a fight, flight, or freeze response.

I saw this phenomenon recently with my seven-year-old daughter, Aly. I told her that she was going to stay the night at her friend Brianna's house, expecting her to get excited. Instead, Aly got angry and said she didn't want to go. Her anger rose, and then she melted into tears.

Knowing something was going on, I asked Aly what she was thinking about. She confessed that the last time she visited Brianna, we informed her we were going to pick her up before dinner. But we hadn't realized how early Brianna's family ate dinner. When they sat down to eat before we came, Aly grew worried and scared. She said she waited by the window for an hour and refused to eat. Not realizing this, John and I had arrived at the time we had planned. We hadn't meant to lie to our daughter or worry her (we had said what we believed would be true). But Aly felt a mix of strong emotions when we didn't show up when she expected—fear, worry, and anger. So when I told Aly she could stay with Brianna again, these same feelings were triggered in her.

Aly's story illustrates what an anger trigger can look like, but in some cases the emotions displayed can be far more intense. Kids with a traumatic background often have this (posttraumatic stress disorder). Some of our children have PTSD, and it helped when their therapist explained that PTSD is more than just a stirring up of memories of past trauma; instead, the sufferer's emotions and body's reaction make her feel as if she's actually reliving that moment. A current trigger can take the child back to all the pain, fear, and anger, causing her body to react as it did the first time, even if she is no longer in that dangerous situation.

For example, I might raise my voice when I discover my child sneaking food, and immediately my child's heart begins to race, her thoughts fill with fear, and her body shuts down. She may not consciously be thinking of all the times when she cried because she was hungry or when she frantically searched the kitchen for food, but her mind and body remember and relive those moments, stirring up immediate anger and a fight for that food.

Sometimes these PTSD episodes include flashbacks, but not always. Emotions that emerge may include fear, worry, sadness, anger, or feelings of being alone and unworthy. Behaviors might involve aggression, and children may even act out parts of the trauma in their daily lives.[1]

When we first adopted our kids, I didn't always understand that their extreme fight, flight, or freeze responses were often related to past trauma. Some responses were obviously related; others less so. During one episode, one of my teen daughters saw a large bug on the floor, and she jumped up on the dining table, screaming and crying so dramatically I was certain she had to be acting. She wasn't. Shocked by her response, I asked her what was wrong, and she screamed at me for not helping her. She seethed, as if I'd put the bug there. I could tell her reaction embarrassed her, but this emotion too came out as anger.

Only after I took care of the bug and allowed my daughter time to calm down could I approach her and help her. It turns out, seeing that bug reminded her of living in a bug-infested home. Seeing the same type of bug took our daughter back emotionally to living in squalid conditions and the terror she felt over not being able to escape the bugs. Yet it wasn't a conscious memory that caused the reaction. Her emotions—her fight-or-flight response—took place even before she realized how she was behaving.

Sometimes I could tell what triggered a fight, flight, or freeze response in my child, but other times not. This is often the case with trauma reminders. Even something as seemingly neutral as an aroma, the sound of a distant train whistle, or a song on the radio can take a child back to a hard place. Our daughter Sissy sometimes froze in the face of a perceived threat. She wouldn't speak and wouldn't respond. Instead, she stared off into space as if replaying a story in her mind. This lasted for a few minutes at a time. Usually I sat by Sissy's side until she returned to the present moment. The anger she exhibited next often surprised me. She'd get mad that I was concerned and that I had asked whether she was all right. Her anger came from not wanting to face the feelings that surged through her. Remember, it can be easier to get mad than to deal with a strong emotion.

If any of this sounds familiar to you or if your child seems to overact in certain situations, it's time to ask questions. Your child may need help dealing with some type of trauma—big or small. If you know of past trauma, seek professional help while your child is young. Ignoring these emotions and behaviors doesn't make them go away. Hopefully some of the tools in this book can provide guidance for how to calm your child and connect with her in ways that will bring healing.

But remember this: not every freak-out moment signifies a trauma trigger. Kids go from zero to ten, from calm to angry, for many reasons. Sometimes mad means sad. It can also mean anxious, afraid, overwhelmed, or any of a variety of emotions. Anger may help a child feel powerful for the moment, but afterward that child usually experiences regret and powerlessness. Anger may temporarily numb the pain, but it doesn't get rid of the hurt.

YOU Are Your Children's Answer

We'll talk about other causes of anger in the next two chapters, but for now let me say that you play a key role in helping your child. Sometimes children need professional help to shift from angry to calm, but they *always* need their parents' help. As difficult as it is to deal with angry kids, this is not a task to turn over to others. Seeking support, especially professional support, may be essential, but it doesn't replace what only you can provide. You are the only dad or mom your kids have. Your kids are reachable, but you have to reach out. Your love, care, affection, and commitment to helping them provide their best chance to live productive and emotionally healthy lives, no matter their ages.

If I had to choose just one thing for you to do while reading this book, it would be to commit. To realize that with God's guidance you can be the help—or find the help—your child needs. Whether you've had your child since birth—or your child is new to your home—you are the expert with your kid. No one is as invested as you are. No one else will deal with the long-range ramifications of your children's emotional health in the same way.

Let your kids know you're on their team when it comes to handling these anger issues. It's not you against your kids; it's you *with your kids* against angry tendencies.

Reflection Questions

1. What truths have you discovered from this chapter about what's really behind "mad"?
2. What response is most common in your kids: fight, flight, or freeze?
3. Why is it easier for your kids—and for you—to be mad than vulnerable?

Action Steps

1. Make a list of things that seem to trigger your child's anger. Add to this list as you go through the week. What do you notice?

2. The next time your child is fighting with you or
   trying to push you away, pause and consider
   whether it's really a cry for you to hold on or draw
   near. Make a plan for how to respond in the future,
   knowing your child really wants you to draw near
   to her.

3. Take note of the next time your child has an
   outburst that seems too dramatic for the situation.
   Later, after your child is calm, create a safe space for
   her to talk and ask her, "What were you thinking
   about when you got mad? Is there another event
   that came to mind, making you mad or upset? Tell
   me about that."

2

ANGER FROM LIFE STRESSORS

There's nothing simple about adding children to one's home. I'm a proactive, organized person, so I assumed the best way to do this was to set up expectations and rules right from the start.

The first day of summer 2015, we picked up our four girls after their last day of school and headed home. As we left the children's home in the background, this new start excited us.

The next day I was ready to find our new norm, and when the girls woke up, I had a list waiting. There were chores to do, bags to unpack, thirty minutes of summer reading, and time blocked out without electronics or television. I felt proud to be so organized, but from the look on the girls' faces this wasn't what they expected. First came the moans and gasps and then the meltdowns.

"We can't even watch television until our room is clean?" one girl spouted.

"Reading? We *have to* read?" her sister complained, crossing her arms over her chest in defiance.

"But you like to read," I objected, noticing that their attitudes were quickly turning angry.

"Yes, but not if I *have to.*"

I looked to Anna, the oldest. She was typically the calm, level-headed one. "This is stupid!" she complained. Her words surprised me. "I can't believe you're doing this to us!" she added. A mix of fear and anger flashed in her eyes, and she rushed up to her bedroom, then slammed the door.

The other girls started arguing, stating which chores they were not going to do. Their voices rose. I stood, feet planted in the kitchen, shocked that things had turned so awful so quickly.

What in the world? What's their problem? A stream of justifications ran through my mind. *We need order in our home or there's going to be chaos. They're not going to just spend all summer zoning out in front of the TV. They need to learn that things will work better with a system.*

"This is stupid!" one of the girls repeated as she scanned the list of books. "I hate this!" Even though she didn't say them out loud, I could almost guess the words to come next. *"Maybe we should just go back now and save ourselves the trouble of things not working out."*

I threw up my hands in frustration. "Forget it! Never mind! Just go … find something to do." The other girls stomped off to join their angry sister. This was not how I expected our daughters' first day in our home to turn out.

It took most of the day to get everyone's anger under control. I wish I could say I gave up on my list immediately, but I still pushed for it. After a few more days of getting the same response, I realized it wasn't going to work. I could not rope these girls into accepting a schedule or developing a routine without anger emerging at every turn.

Only later, as the girls displayed their dismay—sometimes through shouts and sometimes through tears—did I begin to understand. They'd just left an institution with lots of lists, lots of rules, and lots of consequences. Also, the home where they'd experienced a failed adoption had been strict about the same things I'd included on my list. When they saw all my expectations, it caused worry, panic, and fear, all of which the girls exhibited as anger. I'd like to say I learned my lesson that day, but it took me months and months to figure out that life stressors—especially the ones I was causing by pushing for order and structure—were bringing out a lot of anger in my kids.

Looking back, I wish I had just focused on one thing at a time, like a bedtime routine first, then a mealtime schedule, and then chores. I also wish I had focused on the relationships instead of the rules. (Though rules have a place, as we'll discuss later.) I'm learning, though. There is always stuff to teach my kids. I want them to mature as they grow, but I'm learning to take it slowly, with patience and care, just as I would want someone to do with me.

When our kids moved in, they were worried and stressed, wondering how this arrangement would work. John and I also felt some anxiety. They'd never had us as parents before. We'd never had them as kids. Before moving in with us, their home situation had been disrupted time and time again. They were terrified this adoption would fail too, yet they had few skills to deal with the worries that tightened in a ball in their guts.

Even adults can find it challenging to work through intense emotions. But in time we learn that solutions can be brainstormed and schedules can be changed. We learn how to talk to trustworthy people about what's bothering us. But children lack those coping skills. Kids who are oppositional or acting out in angry and aggressive ways often can't explain how they're feeling. They are overwhelmed, yet the only emotion they know how to communicate is anger.

As parents we can help our kids when we better understand what's going on with them, so let's look at the life stressors that can fuel a child's anger.

Feelings of Not Being Heard

Sometimes even when kids communicate their feelings, adults don't listen to what they are saying. We usually have our own agendas, which are focused on order, schedules, and accomplishments, while forgetting that sometimes our kids just want to be kids. They don't want to be a goal or task that we mark off our to-do lists. Children feel frustrated when they are not respected, when parents talk over them, and when they are made to feel as though their interests and ideas aren't important.

"Kids I talk to in therapy say they don't want their parents to yell at them.... They wish their parents would just talk to them," said my friend Cristine Bolley, a licensed professional counselor at Broken Arrow Counseling Services. "And teens are angry because their parents don't believe them when they are telling the truth."[1]

Too often we parents make assumptions about our children's actions and motives. We lecture instead of listening. We always have an answer, instead of stopping to listen.[2]

Impatient or Unsympathetic Parents

On their first morning in our home, I wasn't thinking about my girls' anxiety or their needs. I simply wanted everyone on a schedule. I didn't have patience, realizing that it would take us all time to figure out this new life. I was insensitive to the huge adjustment this was for everyone, including our daughters … who'd grown up in upheaval.

Sometimes, even in everyday life and in ordinary situations, we expect too much of our kids too soon. We desire cleanliness, orderliness, and kindness at all times. It's a standard no adult or child can live up to. And when kids feel helpless to live up to those standards, they get mad. It's even worse when the standards change. "My children get angry having to go back and forth between two separate homes with two totally different sets of rules and discipline," said my friend Heather.[3] Children often get angry when they face situations they can't control.

Unrealistic Expectations

As parents we have dreams of who we'd like our kids to become. But when we expect our children to always earn top grades and to be the best in their sports, we create a heavy burden for them to carry. If they struggle with an activity or class and we push them, it often doesn't help. It just makes our kids mad.

This happened with my son Nathan, who is now an adult. When he was in third grade, I signed him up for rotary basketball. I dropped him off at his first practice, and my sweet and gentle son came out quiet and withdrawn. And then, when the time came for practice a few days later, he didn't want to go. He threw a fit when I told him he had to keep going; he couldn't quit. I thought it was important that he try new things and not give up. I made Nathan keep going, and his attitude just got worse, which was unlike him. He told me he didn't know how to play and all the other kids did. He said they laughed at him. His anger rose as he shared those things, but I thought he just needed a little more time to catch on.

Finally, after a few weeks of Nathan just getting angrier and angrier, I decided to sit in on a practice, and then I understood. To start with, the other boys had been playing together for a few years, and Nathan was new. The coach was calling plays, and all the kids knew where to be and what to do—except Nathan. Not only that, but the other kids *were* teasing him and laughing. Afterward I talked to the coach, but he didn't seem concerned. He brushed me off, and I knew then what I was going to do. When we got to the car, I apologized to Nathan. I also told him that he didn't have to go back. Nathan never showed up to another practice, and no one ever called to ask why. Nathan and I talked about how we should treat others, and I told him that neither the coach nor the kids acted as they should have. We also prayed together—for Nathan, the coach, and those other kids.

I had had unrealistic expectations that Nathan should be able to join a team, learn quickly, do well, and fit in. (In other situations he probably would have.) I thought I needed to teach him to keep going and not give up easily. Instead, what I really needed was to listen to my son. Nathan had tried to talk to me, but it didn't help. No wonder he got mad.

We read in Ephesians 6:4, "Fathers, do not provoke your children to anger by the way you treat them. Rather, bring them up with the discipline and instruction that comes from the Lord" (NLT). We often provoke our kids to anger without really meaning to. We get so focused on what we want or expect that we don't slow down and pay attention to the reasons behind our children's anger. We don't acknowledge that we can often find ways to help, instead of just disciplining them for the ways they act and especially for the ways they act out.

It's not only adults' expectations that can cause kids to become angry; so can their own expectations. For instance, if children expect to be given a toy or a treat every time they go to the store or a test at school will be easier than it turns out to be, they may get angry. Often, when children are used to being the best at something, they become angry if they are suddenly no longer the best.[4] Kids don't know how to handle frustration and disappointment, so they just get mad. And it doesn't help when we tell our kids to just calm down and have a better attitude.

Loss

Many children express anger after a loss, whether it be the loss of a friendship or the death of a pet or family member. "Loss of someone we love cannot be adequately expressed with words," said brain expert Daniel J. Siegel. "Grappling with loss, struggling with disconnection and despair, fills us with a sense of anguish and actual pain. Indeed, the parts of our brain that process physical pain overlap with the neural centers that record social ruptures and rejection. Loss rips us apart."[5]

Anger is one of the normal stages of grief and can be the easiest emotion for a child to express when that child doesn't want to appear vulnerable.

Unsafe People or Unhealthy Relationships

Anger can be a sign of abuse.[6] It is often the only emotion children have to express when they feel unsafe.

If your child seems uncomfortable around a particular person or acts angry when the person is nearby, don't ignore your child's reaction. Instead, press in. Dig deeper to find out why. There *is* a reason your kids are reacting this way. If something in your gut signals there is a problem, then you're most likely right.

My friend's preteen daughter acted awkward and angry whenever an adult male friend came around. Her mother noticed she just wasn't her typical carefree self. After talking with her daughter about her reactions to this man, my friend found out he was treating her daughter inappropriately. The young woman had been scared to tell her parents, but thankfully her mother pressed in, realizing there had to be more behind her daughter's anger.

Let your children know that if they have anything to tell you about something that has happened, you will always believe them. Fear that they won't be believed or uncertainty over what to say or how to talk about what's happening keeps many kids silent. Let your children know you will listen, care, and act.[7]

I'm thankful that I'm learning to see my children's anger as their attempt to communicate with me—so I can understand and help—instead of just seeing it as a behavior problem. It helps me remember that children who act out are in distress and that they don't know how to handle their frustration or anger effectively.

As you can see, numerous things can spark anger in children. In the next chapter, we'll discuss some of the biological reasons children get angry—many of which are often overlooked.

A Humble and Patient Heart

By this point you may be feeling overwhelmed. You may have already identified some situations that are causing or contributing to your child's anger, and you may worry about where to start or how you can help your child. What I do not recommend is for you to jump in and make a lot of changes all at once. I promise you the same thing will happen as what I experienced when I gave my kids their summer to-do list. Your children will feel overwhelmed and sense that *they* are a problem that needs to be fixed, and in the end that will just elicit more anger.

Instead, read through this book with a humble and patient heart. Ask God to show you what changes need to be made first and which you can think about later. Psalm 27:14 says, "Wait for the LORD; be strong, and let your heart take courage; wait for the LORD!" (ESV). Like a gentle shepherd, Jesus will lead you and show you how to best help your kids, in the right way and when the time is right.

You see, this journey isn't just about transforming our kids from angry to calm. It's about allowing God to change us in the process. So many life stressors affect us. Don't let this journey from angry to calm be one of them. Instead, see it as a journey of healing you take with Jesus, trusting and waiting for Him to lead and guide.

Reflection Questions

1. In what angry ways have your kids responded when they felt overwhelmed by life stresses? Is anger the only emotion they exhibit when stressed? How else do they respond?

2. In what ways have you been unrealistic with your expectations or unsympathetic with your kids? How and when has this caused anger?

3. Is there a situation or person that brings up anger or discomfort in your child? What anger cues do you need to be paying attention to? What questions should you ask your child?

Action Steps

1. Sit down with your child and make a list of things in his life that are making him anxious or angry. What surprises you about this list? What changes would he like to make?

2. Make a list of times when you can listen instead of lecturing. During homework? During chore time? Take note of how your child responds when you listen.

3. Ask your child about his angry responses connected to another person. Ask questions like "Tell me about _____. Do you like to be around him/her? Is there something that bothers you about the way he/she treats you? What would you like to tell me?" Ask in a caring, nonconfrontational way.

3

PHYSICAL ISSUES THAT CAN FUEL ANGER

As we've seen, sometimes anger is rooted in trauma and other times in life stressors. But these aren't the only causes of anger in kids.

We were sitting around the table, enjoying lighthearted conversation, when the angry outburst seemed to come from nowhere. Our youngest, Buddy, was a new reader, and he'd been reading aloud to his dad. This sparked a conversation about some of the first books we all remembered reading. John remembered *Mat the Rat*. I remembered reading *Harold and the Purple Crayon*. (Are there even any words in that book?) One of our daughters remembered first reading *Biscuit Finds a Friend*.

"I'm pretty sure one of my first books was *Junie B. Jones*. I learned to read those early," said thirteen-year-old Alexis. And that's when the sister sitting next to her exploded with unexpected anger.

"Why do you have to do that? I hate it when you do that! I'm not stupid!" Rage flashed in Grace's eyes, and all of us looked at her in shock.

"Grace, your sister wasn't trying to make you feel bad. She wasn't comparing herself with you. She simply was talking about what book she first remembers reading."

Grace's eyes were focused on me, but her thoughts were someplace else. Noticing that all the attention around the table was now on her, Grace slumped in her seat and crossed her arms. Heat rose in her face, hinting at the anger still surging inside. After a moment she stood. "Can I be excused?" she asked.

I nodded. "Yes, you may."

As she stomped away from the table, Grace's eyebrows folded down and her lips pressed into a tight line. I wanted to follow and explain again that her sister meant no harm. I also wanted to reprimand Grace for her outburst, but I knew she needed time and space to get ahold of her emotions.

Beyond that, I knew her outburst came from a deep wound she'd been carrying around for years. Grace had learning disabilities and faced a lot of health problems when she was younger, which meant she'd missed a lot of school. The two added together meant that Grace was academically behind other kids her age and that she learned to read late. She was pulled out of class to attend special therapies, and sadly, other kids teased her.

Grace had previously told me, with tears in her eyes, how people used to call her stupid. They'd laughed at her and made fun of her. If that wasn't hard enough, her younger sister learned to read early. Alexis had excelled, while Grace lagged behind. Perhaps some people had compared her with Alexis—or maybe Grace had just done that herself—but hearing Alexis share how she'd learned to read at a young age stirred all those old feelings of shame and embarrassment.

Grace's outburst was not about the present conversation but about the past. Yet she still struggled with feeling inferior. In the middle of our conversation, her emotions had risen so quickly and the outburst had been so unexpected that it surprised everyone, including Grace.

After Grace calmed down, I was able to talk to her about her anger and emotions. She came to understand that Alexis wasn't teasing her. We talked about her old feelings of being "dumb." I reminded Grace of all the ways she excelled, and we talked about how she could handle herself the next time those feeling arose, including coming to talk to me about it. In the end Grace felt much better about herself and gained new tools for how to respond next time.

Grace's feelings about her learning challenges triggered anger in her. In this chapter, we'll look at some of the issues that affect children's moods and bodies in ways that fuel anger: learning disabilities and developmental disorders, sensory processing issues, attention deficit hyperactivity disorder (ADHD), underlying anxiety, food allergies and nutritional or hormonal imbalances, lack of sleep, and lack of order or routine.

Learning Disabilities and Developmental Disorders

If your child is not able to keep up academically, she just may have a learning disability. Kids with learning disabilities and developmental disorders often feel behind and unable to keep pace with others. They may get frustrated and not know how to express their feelings constructively. They don't like feeling vulnerable or inferior, and this often leads to anger.

Children may get angry at other kids when they feel as if they're being labeled as "dumb." They may get upset at teachers for giving them too much work, which they may feel isn't fair. They also may be angry at themselves for not being able to understand what is being taught in the classroom, and they may believe that no matter how hard they try, it will not be enough.

With the right help Grace discovered new ways to learn, but the harder task was helping her not to get frustrated with herself and others. In later chapters, we'll talk about how to teach kids to control their thought patterns and stay calm—even when these types of emotions flare up—but know that this type of anger is common and understandable. None of us like to feel that we are not as smart as others or can't keep up.

Sensory Processing Issues

Many children also get angry when they are overstimulated because of sensory processing issues. These kids have trouble processing the information they receive through their senses from the world around them.

According to the Child Mind Institute, "If your child is over-sensitive, or undersensitive, to stimulation, things like 'scratchy' clothes and too much light or noise can make her uncomfortable, anxious, distracted, or overwhelmed. That can lead to meltdowns for no reason that's apparent to you or other caregivers."[1] A few of my kids have sensory processing issues. They have to wear soft clothes. They cover their ears if noises are too loud. When one child starts to get overwhelmed, he grows angry, and the best thing for me to do is just hold him and give him a huge squeeze. Somehow that's the exact sensory input he needs to calm down.

If a child has sensory processing issues, too much excitement or noise can cause anger to flare up. Case in point: John and I thought taking all our children to Disney World to celebrate their adoptions was a good idea—until we were there. There was just too much input, too much noise, and too much stimulation. This led to many meltdowns, many angry outbursts, and many attempts to get angry children to have fun.

Yet learning about sensory processing issues has helped us parent better. At Disney World we felt at first that we had to keep going. After all, we'd paid a lot of money for the experience. Yet when we realized no one was having fun, John suggested finding a quiet place to have lunch. We spent an hour eating overpriced hamburgers and funnel cakes while our kids fed the birds (something we could have done at the park by our house). But after allowing our kids a little breathing room, everyone calmed down. After that, we decided to follow their much slower pace, and everyone was happier. There was still a lot of stimulation around, but we did our best to take the day slow. Finally by the third day—when we were at Animal Kingdom, a much quieter park—all the kids were able to relax and enjoy themselves.

In the resource section at the back of this book, I've listed some books and websites that helped me better understand sensory processing issues. I know many parents who thought they had an angry kid only to discover they had a child who couldn't handle too much stimulation. It's amazing how a sensory sensitive child's behavior can change when her parents have some tools to quiet her environment.

Attention Deficit Hyperactivity Disorder

ADD (attention deficit disorder) is an outdated term, but it's still used at times. The term currently preferred is *attention deficit hyperactivity disorder*. Key markers of ADHD are hyperactivity and inattentiveness, but some children lean more one way than the other. Symptoms of ADHD include fidgeting, incessant talking, reckless behavior, poor listening and organization skills, being easily distracted, and angry outbursts.[2]

Different children display different symptoms. One of my children, when he's not on his medication, is hyper, loud, and reckless. He'll clap his hands loudly, over and over again, to stimulate himself. Yet one of my daughters also has ADHD, and it is evident simply by her inability to listen and organize information. Children diagnosed with ADHD "may find it very hard to comply with instructions or switch from one activity to another, and that makes them appear defiant and angry."[3]

One doctor explained ADHD in children to me this way: because of a child's unique brain development and chemical makeup, the brain finds comfort through stimulation. If things are too calm, the child must act out—do something—that will stimulate the child. This includes misbehaving, doing repetitive movements, or being impulsive. These children aren't bothered when they upset others; in fact, another person's heightened response may stimulate a child with ADHD.

The doctor went on to say that calm is not comfortable to these kids, but there are medications available that chemically stimulate the brain so children with ADHD won't have to stimulate their brains themselves. The medications pique their brain chemistry—putting them in their comfort zone—so their actions can stay calm.

This explanation helped me understand the importance of medications for my children. It wasn't that they simply needed to learn how to behave or that they were "bad kids." For a child with ADHD, the need for medication has to do with her brain's physical and chemical makeup.

When I shared my concerns about my son's and daughter's behaviors with our pediatrician, she said it sounded like ADHD. We started them both on low doses of medication, and right away I noticed a difference. My daughter started reading, and she was able to keep up. Her angry outbursts happened less and less. My son stopped getting angry to stimulate himself. He stopped picking fights, and we experienced much less anger in our home.

If you feel your child has ADHD, talk to your pediatrician. Your doctor can give you more information and may refer you to a psychiatrist for additional help. Unlike what many people believe, medication for ADHD, if prescribed correctly, does not make children numb or cause them to act like robots. Instead, it provides their brains with stimulation so they can calm their actions, concentrate, stop their anger, and act in appropriate ways.

Underlying Anxiety

Many times children have anxiety because of a stressful situation in their lives, but children with generalized anxiety disorder experience anxiety in the midst of peaceful situations. Generalized anxiety disorder is defined as "chronic, excessive worry and fear." Environmental, physiological, or family factors can cause it. Some children have generalized anxiety disorder because of a chemical imbalance in the brain.[4]

This anxiety often displays itself in unexpected ways. According to the Child Mind Institute, "Children who seem angry and defiant often have severe, and unrecognized, anxiety. If your child has anxiety, especially if she's hiding it, she may have a hard time coping with situations that cause her distress, and she may lash out when the demands at school, for instance, put pressure on her that she can't handle."[5]

When a child is dealing with anxiety, what may seem to be a minor problem can turn into a large outburst. One of our daughters was often anxious about homework. When she came across a problem she didn't understand, her anxiety kicked in and triggered her fight-or-flight instinct—usually the *fight* part. She'd lash out, refuse to do her work, throw her pencils, and verbally attack other people in the room. At first I thought this was simply a behavior problem I had to control, yet when I discovered that anxiety triggered these situations, I turned to other methods: I made her aware I could help her and she didn't need to become anxious. I also taught her to use some calming skills whenever she felt anxiety mounting.

In some children, anxiety is easy to spot; in others, not so much. Signs of anxiety include lots of worried thoughts, trouble sleeping, irritability, and trouble concentrating. I knew one of my teen daughters was dealing with generalized anxiety when she told me,

"I always feel that something bad is going to happen." Unlike her sister's situational cause of homework, this daughter's anxiety was due to a chemical imbalance. When I shared her comment with her doctor, he prescribed a low dose of medication and also advised she see a counselor. The difference we saw in her was huge. Instead of feeling constantly tense and getting angry, she experienced more times relaxing and enjoying life.

Food Allergies and Nutritional or Hormonal Imbalances

Research suggests that foods and food additive sensitivities can induce lack of concentration, overaggressive behaviors, and temper tantrums in adults and children. Poor nutrition has also been linked to inattentiveness, forgetfulness, lack of organization, and impulsivity.[6]

"Food allergies played a large role in my son's moods and his ability to cope with his own emotions," said my friend Kristin. "Gluten is the big one, but sugar and chemical additives are high on the list as well."

"Eating the wrong foods often made my kids angry," said Geri. "Mood swings galore after Saturday morning doughnuts. Angry outbursts and fights. When we got a less sugary breakfast in them, voilà! We had totally different mornings."

Sugar and food dyes affect some children. Gluten and dairy influence others. There are ways to test a child's food intolerances, but the easiest way is to try different foods and then see how they affect your child's behavior. If you discover a few of your child's food triggers, look for resources to help. Start with your child's doctor, and always keep your pediatrician informed of your changes to your child's diet. Further resources are included at the end of this book. Also, I've found that one of the best places to get advice is from other moms who've learned how to make diet changes.

A lack of nutritional balance can also influence children's behavior. Much of our society falls short of reaching the recommended dietary allowance for one or more vitamins and minerals, and this can lead to behavioral problems. Irritability can be caused by vitamin deficiencies, including insufficient amounts of vitamins B, B3, B5, B6, and C.[7] To sum it up, if children don't receive proper nutrition for a long period of time, it can lead to deficiencies that affect their moods and behavior, making some kids extremely irritable or even angry.

As a mother of seven girls, I've also observed another huge physical factor that influences girls' moods as they transform into teens: hormones. Hormone fluctuations in a young woman's body can bring on anger swings. But it is not only preteen and teen girls who struggle with anger due to hormones. Hormones released during puberty create many emotions in both sexes. Puberty can make teens—both girls and boys—unpredictable and irritable.

During adolescence "physical and emotional changes occur at a rapid pace, and the need for acceptance gains importance in a teenager's life. Hormones take over, emotions run high and every teen has to learn how to cope with the new changes. They are also learning to get along with others and discovering their own self-awareness. Learning to adapt to these changes can create anger and sometimes even aggression in some teenagers."[8]

Take note of any reactions in your kids you believe may be due to a food allergy or nutritional deficiency and talk to their doctor about options. As for hormones, I've discovered what works best is lots of physical activity, healthy eating, and a heap of grace. Yet if the anger or aggression reaches the point that the teen wants to hurt herself, harm others, or destroy property, seek professional help.

Lack of Sleep

Growing children need at least nine hours of sleep each night. Toddlers and teens often require more.[9] When children don't get the necessary sleep, they often find themselves unable to deal with their emotions.

While it's sometimes a struggle to get toddlers to bed, it's even harder to get preteens and teens to go to sleep. At this age they often want to stay up late to connect with friends on social media or through texting. They also stay up late to watch movies or play games. This creates a vicious cycle.

"When kids stay up late, their stress hormones like cortisol kick in, which makes it harder to fall asleep," wrote Dr. Laura Markham of Aha! Parenting. "The problem is that cortisol stays in the system and makes them edgy the next day; it also contributes to depression, anxiety, and weight gain. The famous moodiness of teenagers is partly attributable to late bedtimes, which have become standard practice in our culture. Just because your toddler gains the ability to keep himself awake doesn't mean you'd let him stay up half the night. Just because your tween and teen gain the ability to keep themselves up doesn't mean it isn't bad for them."[10] I noticed a big difference in my preteens' and teens' anger issues after we started homeschooling them and they were able to sleep in longer. I know this isn't possible for every child, but if you can find ways for your kids to get more sleep, it can make a world of difference.

Lack of Order or Routine

Some of my children have problems with change. They like to know exactly what's going to happen and when it's going to happen, and when they do, our days go so much better. When things change, especially when they aren't prepared for it, they become anxious and with anxiety comes anger.

My friend Anne's kids are the same. She explained, "Our older kids are pretty laid back. Our youngest does not do well with change of any type. We have to start talking through stuff way in advance with her and continue working with her for weeks afterward."

For some kids, the best way to help them with this issue is to create routines so they will know what to expect. This can include routines for chores, homework, and bedtime. When children know what to expect, they are less likely to get angry when a parent tells them to do a chore or sit down to homework.

With the Right Help

When does your child experience anger? Take note. Pay attention. There's something behind the anger, and if you can figure it out, you're well on your way to helping your kid.

Often we're so busy trying to stop our children's aggression that we don't pause to consider the cause. When we identify what's igniting the anger, we can make changes and help meet our children's needs so they are less likely to act out. Anger clues us into the fact that something is happening within our kids we may need to address.

If any of the issues this chapter touches on ring true as a possible trigger for your child's anger, talk to her doctor about it. Sometimes little changes can bring a huge impact.

I am happy to report that the more attention I pay to my children's needs, the more I've been able to ensure those needs are met, which results in less anger. We still continue to work with Grace and talk with her to show her that the beliefs she had about herself—and that others had of her—do not define her. When I look past the angry moments—and deeper into our daughter's heart—I am better able to identify what help and support she needs.

Also, with the right help and support my teen daughter dealing with generalized anxiety was able to get off most of her medications, including those for anxiety. She has learned coping skills that will allow her to move on to college this year. Because John and I put time and attention into helping her, she doesn't deal with the same anger issues she once did. And that's my hope for all my children. I pray that as we work through the various issues, we are working toward a healthy and independent future for our kids.

Reflection Questions

1. So often we want to immediately control our children's behavior when they are having an angry outburst. In what ways can pausing to take note of the root cause of a child's anger be more important than simply trying to control that child's behavior in the moment?

2. When do your children experience anger? Is it during a certain time of day? Is it after eating certain foods? Is it after a short night's sleep? What stood out to you the most in this chapter about the factors influencing their behavior?

3. How do chemical imbalances in a child's brain contribute to anger? What did you learn from this chapter about such imbalances? How can this knowledge help you help your child?

Action Steps

1. With the information in this chapter in mind, make a list of possible causes for your child's anger. Choose the cause that seems most obvious. Write out one step you can take to find more information or get help from a professional. Also consider seeking advice from another mom who has been able to help her child in this area.

2. If your child is old enough, sit down with her and go over her routine. Is there any part of your child's routine that sparks anger? Talk to your child about the cause of this anger and possible solutions.

3. Choose one food you believe may be prompting anger issues and create a menu that eliminates that food from your child's diet. Keep a journal in your kitchen and take note of what you see.

4

A PARENT'S INTERNAL RESPONSE TO ANGER

The pressure on my chest made sleep difficult. I dreaded waking up the next day, only to deal with my child's anger again. *I'm the worst mom ever. How could I feel this way?*

I grew up in a calm home within a gentle family. There wasn't a lot of drama. As a child, I was cared for. Later, as a wife, I was adored. For most of my parenting years, my kids returned the love I gave them. In my work, I felt appreciated and respected. But now all those feelings of doing a good job or feeling worthy were a distant memory.

The only way to understand what life with an angry child is like is to live through it. The pain of offering love and having hate shot back is heartbreaking. To feed, care for, and serve an angry child is like shoveling coal into a steam engine that has no wheels. No matter how much energy I put into it, a lot of fuel was getting burned, but we weren't going anywhere.

I hated feelings of insufficiency, and I ached with the knowledge that daily I was sacrificing—my time, my work, my friendships, and my personal ease—only to see no good result. Even worse, it seemed the more love I poured out, the more I was ignored.

Even as I write this confession, it almost feels foolish. After all, I'm the adult. I should be able to deal with my emotions, put on my big-girl boots, and keep stepping forward and offering love, right? But maybe you understand. Since you're reading this book, maybe you've been there too. Maybe you're there now. We all want to be loved and respected, but there is something uniquely meaningful about receiving these things back from our kids. Yet many angry kids are so consumed with their anger there is no room for any other emotion, especially love.

Tired of these emotions keeping me awake for days in a row, I took them before God. In the middle of the night, I slipped out of my bed, grabbed my Bible and journal, and poured out all my emotions on the page. I wrote,

> I am hurt by my daughter's rejection. I give so much and to have it rejected hurts. I feel abandoned and not good enough. I can't fix this. I can't fix her. I worry about the other kids. I want to be loved by her, and I want to love her. I'm tired of being hurt. I feel angry to sacrifice so much, and instead of gratitude I get defiance and rejection in return.

It felt cleansing to get those words on paper. I'd carried around those emotions for so long, but seeing them—the deep pain my child's anger caused me—made me understand why everything had been so hard lately. It's not easy to go on with your life—trying to be happy, caring, and giving—with so much emotion bottled up inside.

Yet even as I looked at what I had written, I heard a still, small whisper from God: *Ask Me how I see her.* I knew what God was asking me to do—to view this situation through His eyes, with His eternal perspective.

As I gazed at those words on my page, it was not only my heart cry that I saw there but also my child's. I wrote this in my journal next:

> She is afraid of being hurt. She's given so much to oth-
> ers, and her heart is battered. She has been abandoned.
> She has been told she's not good enough. She couldn't
> fix anything about her family or where she lived. She
> wants to love me and be loved by me, but she's afraid.
> No matter what she gets, she's scared it will be taken
> away. She wants to reject me before she is rejected.

As I wrote those words, I knew they were the truth, and I chose to continue to reach out to my daughter through loving actions, no matter how she responded. I prayed that God would soften and open my heart. I prayed He would help me show her my love in ways she'd understand. As I prayed this way and began to show love in ways that spoke to my daughter, things changed. I started looking forward to trying to connect with her emotionally, and I watched the walls around her heart crumble and her anger diminish. And it all started with my heart. In order to help my child, I first needed to focus on myself.

The Heart of the Matter

The truth is, as parents of angry kids, we need to truly get to the heart of the matter—our hearts. We cannot help our child if we keep our own anger, disappointment, and frustration sealed up inside. Have you been bottling your own anger as you've been dealing with your angry kids? The first step is to admit it. Take time to get by yourself and quiet your spirit. Ask God to help you understand what's really going on within you. Know that God loves you and wants to help you understand your own anger and the healing He can bring.

Some of the roots of your anger may be a sense of injustice, strife, weariness, unmet needs, or impatience. Take time to write out what you're really feeling. If your feelings are similar to mine, you might write something like this:

> It's not fair that I'm the one having to deal with my child's anger issues. Every little problem turns into a big conflict. I'm weary from dealing with the anger day after day. I can't spend my time as I want to or need to because I'm spending so much time just trying to help my child. Sometimes I feel like throwing up my hands and giving up. I'm at the end of my rope.

Next, take your emotions before God. He's not surprised by them. He's more aware of your emotions than you are. Also, know that occasional anger isn't a sin—acting out on that anger in inappropriate ways is. Know too that holding that anger inside doesn't help anything either. It clouds your thinking about every situation, especially those that involve your child. To quote an old German proverb: "Fire in the heart sends smoke into the head."

Getting my emotions on paper gave me things to think about and pray about for myself. Instead of feeling God's disapproval, I sensed Him asking me to release the anger in order to change my thinking. He wanted me to look at my daughter differently. He wanted me to see her as He did … as someone who was also hurting. As someone who was trying to reject me before she was rejected. While I knew God wanted me to work on my anger, I also felt His love in that moment. He knew my struggle and wanted to heal me and my relationships.

That morning with my Bible and journal, as morning larks' songs filtered through the window, I prayed God would give me His heart for my daughter. I asked Him to help me love her in all the ways she needed me to—even in ways I might not fully understand. And in those moments of prayer, things changed. I started to feel differently toward my daughter. So much so that when she walked downstairs that day into the living room where I was sitting, I didn't tense up. Instead, I hurried toward her and asked whether I could give her a hug. She must have sensed the difference in me, because she didn't hesitate. She opened her arms.

As I wrapped her up in my arms, *I* changed. It's not that I no longer struggled but that my care for my daughter grew despite the struggles. The seeds of God's compassion planted inside me changed my perspective. Looking at what was behind my anger—and behind my daughter's anger—helped me see there was heart work to be done.

I wonder, Could the same be true for you? Could the struggle you are having with your child be the very thing God wants to use to bring you and your child together, just as He did for me and my daughter?

Instead of viewing anger as a *problem* your child will have to deal with his whole life, understand that anger provides an *opportunity* for you to work with your child to better himself. (And better yourself in the process.) Your child's anger is the warning light that tells you some maintenance is needed on your child's heart and with your child's behavior. Anger is a welcome mat inviting you to enter your child's world, seek out his heart, build a relationship, and figure out what's really going on.

No family is perfect. We live in a fallen world. If anger causes us to depend on God more and grow in our relationship with our kids, then it's worth it. And it all starts with sitting before Him, asking Him to change hearts … which will then begin to change our thoughts. And changed thoughts, as we know, change everything.

Dealing with My Own Anger

Have you ever paused to consider what triggers your anger? (Notice that I didn't ask *whether* your anger is triggered. I asked *what* triggers it.) Understanding those triggers is an important step to knowing how to control it. For most of us, anger starts with our thoughts and the emotions that come with them. For example:

- When the house is a mess after I worked hard to clean it, I feel unseen or unheard and I think, *No one even sees or cares about all the work I do around here. They don't listen when I ask for help.*

- When one of my angry kids ruins something I have or own, I feel powerless and I think, *My kids are going to ruin all my stuff. I'm never going to be able to have nice things.*
- When my child's anger seems uncontrollable, I fear the future and I think, *He's going to get kicked out of school with that temper. Then what am I going to do?*

If you find yourself becoming emotional when your child is angry, pause and identify the thought that comes with the emotion. Usually the thought ties back to something in your past or projects difficult times ahead in the future. It also could be projecting how you look—or how your child looks—to others.

Do you feel yourself getting angry because your child having a fit in the grocery store embarrasses you? Your thought might be, *All these people are going to think I'm a bad parent.*

Do you feel yourself getting frustrated when your child's homework angers him? Your thought might be, *This is taking too long. We're going to be up late, and I won't get enough sleep for my big presentation tomorrow.*

After you determine what your thoughts are, consider how accurate and useful they are. If a thought simply fuels your anger, it's not helpful. But it is possible to change that thought to one that is more accurate or helpful.

For example, if your child throws a fit in the store, you can think, *My guess is that every parent has gone through this. We'll get through it too.*

Or if your child is getting frustrated with his homework, you can think, *If I stay calm, he'll be able to calm down; then we can work through this together and finish more quickly.*

Changing our thoughts in such situations takes practice, and we won't always get it right, but when we replace the thoughts that lead to our anger, we can become more sympathetic with our children. We can also help them with the thoughts that lead to their anger. (We'll talk more about how to do that in a later chapter.)

"Imperfections are not inadequacies; they are reminders that we're all in this together. Imperfectly, but together," wrote shame expert Brené Brown.[1] Just because your child handles anger imperfectly now doesn't mean he can't learn. And just because you're handling your child's anger imperfectly now doesn't mean you can't learn either. Don't let your thoughts take control and make you feel as though all is hopeless. After all, you are the one who controls your thoughts. You get to choose which thoughts stay and which go. You can choose the story and the dialogue.

I may start to think, *My child's anger is getting on my nerves and making me angry.* But then I pause, blow out a breath, and rephrase that thought. *This is my opportunity to help my child. I will stay calm. I will do my best to help my child with God's help.*

Changed Thoughts, Changed Actions

Like most moms, I have a plan in my mind about how things should go. When I clean my house, it should stay clean. When I tell my kids it's time to leave, they should put on their shoes and get in the car. When I sit down to help my children with homework, they should pay attention and work quickly. Yet things don't always go that way. Instead, my kids make messes and then get angry when I ask them to clean up. They get mad when we have to leave the house because they're in the middle of watching a movie. They get upset with homework and complain it's not fair that they have so much. I'm not sure why I'm often surprised and upset when my kids get angry, but I am. And episode after episode builds my frustration and the anger I hold inside.

Controlling my thoughts means not expecting everything to go right and instead knowing things that don't go as planned will fill each day. Instead of getting frustrated and angry about those things, I chose to do two things. First, I chose to become more realistic about my expectations and standards and not get so frustrated and angry. And second, instead of feeling helpless, I chose to work on systems that could help my kids. I decided to be proactive instead of reactive.

What types of systems? I started to change things *one at a time*: chore charts, mealtime routines, bedtime routines. I trained my kids to do better, instead of just getting frustrated and mad when their actions didn't meet my expectations. With systems in place, my house wasn't as messy and my kids didn't complain as much about every little thing. They weren't perfect, but since I was also working at being more realistic, I was less frustrated and angry as I remembered that together we were doing our best.

It's not that I did this perfectly either, but whenever overwhelming emotions built within me, I'd try to pause and think, *Okay, my emotions are telling me there is a problem. First, what is the problem? Second, how can I fix this? Or instead of fixing it, do I just need to relax and not get so worked up about this today?*

Sometimes the fix meant creating or reevaluating a system or schedule. Other times it meant being creative with finding a solution. Very quickly my thinking began to change.

Before: *This place is such a mess. I can't believe my kids treat me this way.*

After: *This place is such a mess. We're going to have to do a fifteen-minute family cleanup before dinner.*

Before: *This kid's attitude stinks. I don't deserve that attitude.*

After: *This kid's attitude stinks. I'm going to pull him aside for one-on-one time after dinner.*

Then sometimes I just had to let things go: *This place is such a mess, but it's been a busy time for all of us. I'll worry about this tomorrow. Today, I'm just going to let my anger and frustration go and focus on my kids.*

Or: *This kid's attitude stinks, but I don't need to let it affect my attitude too. It's a good day, and God has given me so much. His attitude is something we'll continue to work on over time.*

Can you see the difference a change in thought patterns makes? As I changed my thinking, I realized I was in control, instead of feeling helpless. I developed systems, and I became proactive. I chose how to respond, instead of just piling up all my negative emotions inside. Of course, that doesn't mean I always get it right. That's where confession comes in.

Confession Opens Us Up to Our Kids

Like anything else, changing worried, anxious, and angry thoughts to thoughts of peace takes time. Change happens, though, when we make a conscious effort to do so—and when we evaluate ourselves at the end of each day to see how well we've done. "Did I offer peace today? Did I bring a smile to someone's face? Did I say words of healing?" asked author Henri Nouwen. "Did I let go of my anger and resentments? Did I forgive? Did I love?"[2] We need to ask ourselves similar questions—and then be willing to talk with our kids about our own struggles with anger and frustration.

One of the best ways for our kids to learn how to handle their anger is for them to hear us confessing the areas where we mess up—and to see how we're trying to change. I confess when I've been frustrated or angry. I confess when I raise my voice or talk rudely. I confess when my expectations are too high. I confess when I don't make time for my kids and instead fill my time with so many other things it leaves them frustrated and needy. And after my confession, I ask for my children's forgiveness.

Of course, sometimes I don't wait to confess or ask for forgiveness. Many times I ask immediately—in the moment—and then I bring it up again later in our family's devotional time. I explain how I've messed up and how I'm turning to God to help me, and then I usually share a verse that illustrates how I am seeking God's help. For instance, I might say, "James 1:19 says, 'Everyone should be quick to listen, slow to speak and slow to become angry.' And I haven't done a good job of doing that. I haven't listened. I'm sorry I got angry. I'm praying God will give me more patience." The more I'm willing to humble myself, the more my kids are willing to do the same.

Confession isn't easy. It's hard to peel back our layers and share our true selves, even with our families. But as hard as it is to confess our shortcomings, that confession is what our kids need. They need to know we struggle too. They need to know there's more behind a parent's anger than what they can see—otherwise they might think *they* are the problem.

So be honest with your kids when you mess up and act out in angry ways. Don't try to justify yourself. You're not fooling them. Instead, model for them how to repent and how to ask for forgiveness when you have messed up. And turn to God for help in dealing with your own anger toward your children.

The Pathway to Healing

God doesn't want us to have to carry around regret for our emotions, thoughts, or actions. He doesn't want us to hold grudges against our kids or harbor bad thoughts toward them. He wants us free from our anger and all the things that trigger it. The closer we draw to God, the more He can help us.

Where can the healing begin? It starts in these three ways.

First, understand forgiveness. Forgiveness is placing the wrong in God's hands. It's forgiving others and ourselves. Colossians 3:13 says, "Make allowance for each other's faults, and forgive anyone who offends you. Remember, the Lord forgave you, so you must forgive others" (NLT). When we turn over our children's shortcomings—and our own—to God, it gives Him the chance to work as only He can.

Second, welcome the Holy Spirit. Galatians 5:16 says, "So I say, let the Holy Spirit guide your lives. Then you won't be doing what your sinful nature craves" (NLT). When we welcome the Holy

Spirit into our lives, He can help and guide us. He will be present as we work through our emotions, thoughts, and actions, leading us to freedom. He can remind us He is there to help. The Holy Spirit can also guide us in helping our kids, stirring our hearts as we read God's Word and open ourselves to His still, small voice throughout the day.

Third, fill your mind with God's truth. Second Timothy 3:16–17 says, "All Scripture is inspired by God and is useful to teach us what is true and to make us realize what is wrong in our lives. It corrects us when we are wrong and teaches us to do what is right. God uses it to prepare and equip his people to do every good work" (NLT). When God's truth fills our mind, we will be able to see the numerous areas in our lives where God wants to work. And when we allow His Word to work within us, we're also opening ourselves up to do the good work that God has prepared us to do—in this case, helping calm our children and helping them manage their anger.

While determining what areas of our lives need healing can be difficult at times, God's truth and God's Spirit can penetrate our hearts. The question *What makes me angry?* provides a starting point as we search for areas we need to open up so God can work in them. It's more than a question. It's the first step toward a pathway to healing. When we willingly go before God, His Spirit will bring realizations, confessions, and forgiveness to the forefront. God knows we need healing and wholeness within ourselves and within our relationships with our kids. And the more we work with Him in dealing with our internal response to anger, the better able we'll be to love and draw closer to our kids.

Reflection Questions

1. How can putting your angry thoughts about your child on paper—and asking God to help you see your child as He does—change your heart and attitude?

2. Why do we often forget that we have control of our thoughts? What would change if you saw your thoughts of frustration and anger as opportunities to make changes and draw closer to your kids?

3. Why are confession and seeking forgiveness important parts of dealing with anger?

Action Steps

1. Sit before God. Write down the emotions you're feeling concerning your angry child. Ask for His opinion about your child. Ask Him to give you His heart for your child.

2. Think of something within your home, such as chores or homework, that brings frustration and anger to both you and your child. Think of a system you can set in place to help you conquer this together.

3. Write a prayer concerning the current anger struggles within your home. Ask God to show you how these things can be opportunities to bring you and your child closer to each other and to Him.

5

A PARENT'S EXTERNAL RESPONSE TO ANGER

When we are angry at our kids, we often respond similarly to how our parents responded in anger to us. During my growing-up years, my stepdad went from calm to slap-you-on-the-side-of-the-head angry in fifteen seconds flat. I found myself repeating that cycle. Most of the time I dealt with my children's disobedience in a peaceful manner, and then something small would push me over the edge and I'd get mad. I wouldn't hit, but flicks to the shoulder, smacks on the hand, or a firm squeeze on my child's arm let my child know I was serious.

Then one day I realized I was following in my stepdad's footsteps. I was sitting next to my son while he colored. I moved to swipe his bangs out of his eyes and he flinched. His fear broke my heart. I offered a loving gesture, but that wasn't what my son expected. After that, I began to work on stopping those angry actions. I turned to God and prayed about my anger. If I felt frustration building, I'd count to ten and then offer up a quick prayer that God would help me not respond in anger. I'm thankful my older kids can't remember that angry mom.

But eighteen years later, after adding more kids to our home, I struggled again with those same angry emotions and actions. This time my anger didn't dissipate after I counted to ten and prayed. This time my children continued to push my buttons and tried to get me to jump on their anger bandwagons, even as I fought to stay calm.

Now my goal is to try to stay calm and let my face, tone, and words reflect that. I'm learning how to breathe deeply, hold in my frustration, and exhale. I try to relax my face and soften my features. When tension builds, instead of lowering my voice in anger, I raise my voice an octave, trying to sound softer and more understanding. And I pray, pray, pray.

When it comes to anger, we can always do better. We will get angry. We will become frustrated. But how we handle ourselves is up to us.

Here are some ways we can maintain control and not react in anger and frustration.

Don't Join Every Fight You're Invited To

Why do our kids get in our faces when they get mad? It's an invitation for us to join them. They want us to engage and escalate with them. Why? First, when we escalate with our children, they feel justified. If we *get* angry, then they can *stay* angry. Anger feeds more anger, and in the moment it's a powerful feeling for our kids. Second, when our children are angry and we get angry at them, then *they become the victims*. Suddenly they're crying because of our behavior.

One of my children was especially good at being a victim. When she did something wrong, she'd poke at me or one of her siblings (with words or actions) to get one of us worked up. Then, when the other person got angry, she'd retreat and cry. In the past, people went to her "rescue" to comfort her. The fact that she had acted wrongly and in anger was ignored. (Smart kid!) When I talked to her therapist about this issue, the therapist agreed this was a bad cycle that needed to be broken; otherwise my daughter would grow up and always find ways to be the victim.

I knew this behavior needed to be stopped. So how? By my not becoming angry back, no matter how my daughter pushed. No matter what my daughter said or did, I was onto her "game," and I did my best to remain calm. I worked to disengage my own emotions and tell myself, *I don't want her to become a victim, and I'm not going to join in her drama.*

It worked. As I stayed calm, my daughter learned that provoking me wasn't going to work, and she stopped trying. I also taught the other kids to recognize when someone was trying to pull them into a fight. I'd say, "Your sibling is trying to pull you in and make you angry. Don't let them win." It didn't always work. Sometimes they still joined the fight. But once they realized what was happening, they were drawn in less and less.

Don't Escalate with Your Child

When our children are angry and their emotions are rising, it's easy for ours to do the same. The thing is, when we escalate, our children often raise their anger to exceed ours. Soon no one is in control.

Sometimes becoming angry has become a bad habit. Other times we just want to get our kids to do what we say. Sometimes we simply want to win the fight. (Who doesn't want to win?) Yet we parents win when we stay controlled. When we stay calm, our kids are able to calm down more quickly. When we stay calm, we can think clearly. We maintain control, and we make good choices about how we act, what we say, and how we discipline. More than that, by remaining calm, we are positive role models for our kids. After all, how can we tell our kids to control themselves when we're not willing to do the same?

As author Robert Fulghum said, "Don't worry that children never listen to you; worry that they are always watching you."[1] It is no coincidence that the first thing our infant children are able to focus on is our faces as we cradle them. By God's design we are supposed to be the first—and most important—influence in our children's lives. They watch, and they learn. They determine how to act by how we act and react.

I can't tell you the number of times one of my teen daughters approached me and said something like, "I don't know how you do it. I'm not sure how you stay so calm when she [meaning a sister] is acting like that." Comments like this usually come after I've just dealt with one of the other kids in the middle of an angry moment. I usually share the tools I've learned with the watching, observant child. During these times, I'm also able to express this truth: "It's not me; it's Jesus. When I lean on Him and depend on Him, everything changes. He works in me and through me and gives me wisdom and strength."

This is what our kids need to see—us dealing with an angry child and maintaining control. Being able to deal with angry people and hard situations is a necessary part of life.

What do your children see during an angry moment? Would you want them to follow your actions? "First and foremost, we need to be the adults we want our children to be," wrote Brené Brown. "We should watch our own gossiping and anger. We should model the kindness we want to see."[2] When we are kind, even when everything inside us wants to be anything but kind, our kids take notice.

It's not easy. I still struggle to keep calm when dealing with a defiant, disobedient child, especially one who mouths off or interrupts me. Because I struggle with this, I've asked friends for their advice on how they handle angry kids. Here are some of their recommendations:

- "Stare at them and ask if they need a hug."
- "I try to remember that a child who feels safe enough to be angry around me feels safe with me, and that's not something I want to violate. I also had my kids memorize Ephesians 6:4 when they were little. Knowing they know that verse has been wonderful accountability. We also teach them Ephesians 4:26: 'Be angry, and yet do not sin' (NASB). That gives us a foundation for when the anger gets the better of them to address the behavior rather than the emotion."

- "When I was a teacher, I'd pretend I was being
  filmed for a video to demonstrate what to do for
  other teachers."

My friends are so wise! I love these tips. I especially love the idea
of pretending someone else is watching me in order to help me better handle a situation. I always act more appropriately—speak more
appropriately—when I know I have an audience, whether it's my
spouse, neighbor, or friend from church. And this tells me one thing: I
can control myself and my words. If I can do so when I believe others
are listening, I can do so even when I know they're not.

Control Your Words and Your Body

I can come up with a dozen sarcastic things to say when I'm angry,
but I always regret what I say in anger. I still remember things my
parents said to me when they were angry—things they probably
didn't mean. And I know I've said things in anger that hurt my children. That's why it is so important for us parents to learn to seal our
lips so we don't say the wrong thing.

We also need to work on saying the right things. When one of
my children is angry, instead of escalating with her, I try to use some
of these phrases:

- "I see you're angry."
- "I am sorry that hard thing happened to you. I'll
  be here to talk about it when you're ready."

- "When things like that happen, I get angry too. How can I help?"
- "When you're ready, I can tell you how I handle it when I get mad."
- "It's okay to be angry, but watch how you act next. Make a good choice."
- "I understand you're angry. Do you want to try to understand my point?"

I've discovered that when I acknowledge my children are angry, it helps them see that I'm paying attention. Also, when I make myself available, my kids often turn to me for help. They want to make good choices; they just need some extra support to do it.

I wish I could say I always get it right, but I don't. Sometimes the right thing is for me to admit I'm wrong or to apologize for not paying attention when I needed to. Sometimes I don't want to engage and help my children. Sometimes I just want to send them to their rooms. Sometimes I simply want to ignore the problem and pretend it's not happening. (There are eleven people who live in our home, and I've gotten good at blocking out noise.) Yet I'm learning that the sooner I apologize for my part in the problem (not listening to my children, for example), the sooner my children are willing to calm down, which allows me to help them with their anger.

Often my responses surprise my kids—when I really want to help instead of simply sending them to their rooms or giving them consequences. As I mentioned before, six of my adopted children experienced trauma. To them adult anger meant hurt, meant pain.

It's nothing any child should ever have to face. As adults it's our job to control our words and actions.

It goes without saying that as parents we must never use our bodies to control or inflict injury on our child in our anger, but there's another way we need to control our bodies that most people don't think about, and that's calming them when we feel frustrated or angry. For instance, if I feel my jaw tightening, I know it's time to relax it. When my brow furrows, that's my cue to soften my facial features. If my hands are clenched in preparation for verbal sparring, I pause and open them. It's a sign I'm releasing the anger and I'm opening up to finding a solution and seeking God's help to do so. The physical opening of my hands somehow relaxes my whole body.

As you can see, sometimes less is more. Fewer emotions, fewer words, fewer reactions. And sometimes the best thing parents can do is ignore the angry behavior completely.

Ignore the Behavior

About six months after we brought our oldest adopted children home, we were still struggling with one of our daughters getting angry at night and causing a lot of drama. This was more than just her being tired and grumpy. It was as if she was purposefully picking fights to cause a big scene.

Of course, we had to deal with it, so John and I were usually up an hour after our daughter's bedtime, dealing with her anger and trying to get her to bed. It was no fun. There were a lot of emotions and drama. John and I often collapsed into bed far more exhausted than we had been an hour before.

When we talked to our daughter's therapist about what was happening, she told us it sounded as if our daughter was seeking attention. When she acted in angry ways before bedtime, she received a lot of individual attention from Mom and Dad. The therapist suggested we ignore it the next time our daughter tried to use anger to create drama. Because most of the anger was directed at us, this would be easier to do since we didn't have to worry about her acting out against the other kids.

The drama happened again that very night. Our daughter was mad at us about something, but instead of engaging with her, John and I moved into the kitchen to talk. John sat on a barstool, and I leaned against the counter, facing him. Although our daughter raged close to us in the living room, we gave her no direct attention. Instead, we just started talking about our day as if we didn't have a care in the world.

Seeing that her attention-seeking ways weren't working, our daughter marched into the kitchen and got out a barbecue lighter from a high cabinet. At that time none of our kids were allowed to play with fire or light candles. With all the issues going on, it just wasn't safe. Knowing this, our daughter announced, "I'm going to light *all* the candles in the house."

Still we ignored her.

From where we sat, we could indeed hear her walking around the house, lighting all the candles. Though we remained on subtle alert for any real danger, we continued to talk about our day (probably repeating the same things we'd already said).

When our daughter saw that she was still not getting our attention, the threats started. She said things like "Oh, what if I dropped this candle? It might catch the house on fire" and "Oh, I wonder if you'd be able to get all the kids out of a burning house."

Seeing that we still weren't giving her attention, she placed the candle back on the shelf.

Despite her actions, John and I continued to talk and maintain eye contact. Every time I started to tense up, John lifted a brow and whispered, "Stay calm." And every time he started to tense up, I did the same.

After fifteen minutes had passed and our daughter still wasn't getting our attention, she turned to the one thing she guessed *would* get my attention: ruining my books. Not just any books, but the brand-new, very expensive homeschool books that had just arrived. From where we sat, we could hear her in the other room. "Oh, look at these books. They look very important and expensive." And then I heard a sound that still causes a shiver to race down my spine: *rip, rip, rip.*

I straightened up, and John motioned for me to stay calm. I acted calm on the outside, but inside my heart raced. After a few minutes of ripping, I knew she would continue her show as long as she thought we could still hear her. At that point both John and I announced we were going to bed. We walked right past her, without even giving a side glance, and went to our bedroom. Within a minute, the ripping of books stopped, and we heard her walking upstairs to her room. The drama had ended. We hadn't given in. But had it worked?

John slipped out of our room ten minutes later and blew out all the candles, and when he returned, he looked tired and sad. "There are ripped book pages all over the living room," he informed me.

"I'll deal with it tomorrow," I said as I crumpled into bed.

When I opened my eyes the next morning, the damaged books were the first thing I remembered. Hurrying into the living room, I stopped before all the torn pages, shocked. Our daughter had ripped up notebook paper, not book pages. All my schoolbooks were still in the box, unharmed.

I couldn't believe it. She'd "acted out," but she'd done so with a degree of restraint, something I hadn't expected. I never mentioned the episode to her, and I waited until that night to see whether we were going to have a repeat performance. Amazingly that evening when we told her to go to bed, she did. Obviously it was no fun staying up and being dramatic when she didn't get the attention she sought.

I tell this story to illustrate what I've learned. Sometimes kids seek our attention through anger or acting out because they feel it's the only way to get attention from us. Yet when we don't give our kids the attention their angry behaviors seek, they'll often stop doing those behaviors. And when we take the next step—to empathize with our children—not only can it stop an angry episode, but it can also help our children feel as if they're understood.

Empathize with Your Child

"Sincere empathy works wonders," wrote Jim Fay and Charles Fay. "Sarcastic empathy backfires every time."[3] This means pretending to be empathetic will backfire.

It's hard being a kid, and sometimes the best way I can help during an angry episode is to listen to my child and validate her feelings.

I can let her know that I am sad along with her, frustrated along with her, and even angry along with her. I can grieve with a child when her toy is broken. I can feel disappointment with her when she gets a bad grade on a test. I can be mad about a bully. By empathizing with my child, I help her see that her feelings are acceptable even though harmful behavior is not.

Why is empathy important? Because when a child no longer has to defend her feelings, she can move on and release them. And we can be there to help.

But if we tell our kids their feelings don't matter or they were wrong to feel that way, then they will keep being angry. If we ignore our kids' underlying emotions, we'll never get to the root of their anger. They will continue to lose control and lash out because they want us to know this *is* a serious matter to them. Our children will continue to get mad because no one takes their feelings seriously. They will lose their tempers easily because they haven't released all the junk piled up inside them.

The more I try to put myself in my children's shoes, the more I'm willing to empathize with them. And the more I empathize with them, the more I'm willing and able to help them.

As you have probably realized by now, I believe a large part of helping our kids is dealing with ourselves—first. How we, the parents, act makes all the difference. When we let our anger get the best of us, it'll just fuel the fire in our kids. When we get mad at our children's anger and act out, nothing will change. It'll only get worse.

The good news is that as we work on our responses, our habits, and our angry actions, our kids will benefit. They will know they can trust us to help them with their anger because they'll see how we are actively handling ours.

I'm thankful I'm overcoming the angry responses I saw modeled during my growing-up years. It was a cycle worth breaking. And now I'm hoping that my positive actions are creating a cycle worth following for my kids. I want them to be able to control their anger, now and as adults. I want them to know I'm here to help them do just that. And it all starts with the way I model and teach my kids how to do things right, with self-control and empathy.

Reflection Questions

1. How did your parents—or other role models—deal with anger? How did this affect how you deal with anger as an adult?
2. What helps you stay calm when you are angry? What is the best advice you've received to help you stay calm?
3. How does escalating in anger with your child hurt you in the end?

Action Steps

1. Do you find yourself dealing with a child who acts dramatic and angry in order to get attention? Choose ahead of time to ignore that child's behavior. Don't let the drama get you worked up. Write down what you did and what happened.

2. When your child is angry, instead of escalating with your child, say some of the following:

   - "I see you're angry."
   - "I am sorry that hard thing happened to you. I'll be here to talk about it when you're ready."
   - "When things like that happen, I get angry too. How can I help?"
   - "When you're ready, I can tell you how I handle it when I get mad."
   - "It's okay to be angry, but watch how you act next. Make a good choice."
   - "I understand you're angry. Do you want to try to understand my point?"

3. Next time your child is sad, frustrated, or angry, try to empathize with your child's feelings. Let your child know you want to understand and you care.

Part 2

HELPING YOUR ANGRY KID

6

BUILDING BONDS

I was standing at the stove, putting leftovers into containers, when I noticed my teen daughter trudging out of the room.

"Hey there. Don't slip out so fast. You have kitchen chores this morning."

A grumpy moan escaped her lips. "Uh, do I have to now ... Can't I do it later?"

"No. I don't want to leave the kitchen like this. Please unload the dishwasher while I put this food away."

A moment later cabinet doors began slamming and dishes clattered.

Two of the younger kids ran through the room, laughing and screeching.

"Get out of here!" their older sister shouted. "You're in my way!"

"Listen now—don't treat them that way."

"But I'm tired." She stomped across the kitchen. "I haven't been sleeping good lately!" Her words were loud and harsh.

"Listen." I placed a hand on my hip. "This is the first I heard about you not feeling well. If you're having a problem with sleep, we can discuss it, but this is no way to act. You need to find a way to control your anger."

I admit I wasn't as compassionate as I could have been. I just wanted the kitchen clean. I turned back to the leftovers and then suddenly felt arms circling me. My daughter had pulled me into a hug. I embraced her back, and she sank into my arms. In that moment I remembered a few things. She wasn't happy with her behavior any more than I was. She wanted to change, but she needed help. She needed my touch—and a connection with me to move past her anger.

I held my daughter, hugging her tight, and told her I loved her. I also told her I was sorry she was feeling tired. An apology spilled out of her lips, and we stood there for a minute, enjoying the resolution after a tense moment. I realized then how much easier it would have been if I had offered care and comfort right from the start, even though she was acting rude and angry.

Instead of rushing off to do other chores, I stayed and rinsed all the breakfast dishes to make loading the dishwasher easier for her. We talked as we worked, and when we were done, my daughter smiled and thanked me for the help. Then she went to her siblings and apologized for her attitude. My daughter had known what she needed even more than I did: a little compassion, a little care, and—in this case—a great big hug.

More Connection, Less Anger

Aren't compassion and tenderness what we all want, and aren't we less angry when we get them? As a wife I know that I get along best (and get less angry) with my husband when we've had time to connect.

"Scientists have found a way to predict which couples will end up divorcing: those who don't insure that they have at least five positive interactions for every negative one. According to John Gottman of the Gottman Institute, it is likely that maintaining this 5 to 1 ratio is effective insurance in every relationship, including between parents and children," wrote Dr. Laura Markham. "Try as we might, all of us sometimes have less than optimal interactions with our children. Remember that each one of those interactions that leave anyone feeling bad require five positive interactions to restore a positive valence to the relationship. These can be little—a smile or pat on the shoulder—as long as you make sure they have a positive impact."[1]

Usually, with my kids, the negative interactions involve me focusing on the rules over the relationship: such as making sure my kids do their chores or finish their homework, instead of taking time to connect with them first. When I first take time to have a positive interaction with them, such as making eye contact and asking about their day or offering a hug, I'm less concerned about the rules. They just don't matter as much. I'm able to see my kids' needs, instead of simply seeing a task that needs to be done or a rule that needs to be followed. Amazingly, doing this actually means the goals behind the rules end up being achieved more easily and naturally in the long run.

That was the case when my daughter stepped forward to embrace me. Even though I had been focused on the task that needed to get done, her gesture reminded me of my daughter's heart and needs. When I hugged her back, we had a positive interaction that built a connection in our relationship. After that hug, I stayed to help her with her chore, which gave us time to talk. (Vital one-on-one time and task completed all at once!) Because of that hug, what started as a negative interaction turned into a positive one.

When we spend time with our kids—and connect with their hearts—fewer anger issues will arise. Yet the importance of connecting with our kids is more than that. When our kids connect with us, they learn how to read other people's feelings and emotions. Dr. Amy Banks explained,

> A good example of [humans being hardwired to connect] is mirror neurons, which are located throughout the brain and help us read other people's feelings and actions.... When two people are in conversation they are stimulating each other's mirror neuron system. Not only will this lead to movement in similar muscles of the face (so the expressions are similar) but it also allows each to feel what the other is feeling. This is an automatic, moment to moment resonance that connects us. There have been studies that look at emotions in human beings such as disgust, shame, happiness, where the exact same areas of the brain light up in the listener who is reading the feelings of the person talking. We are, literally, hardwired to connect.[2]

If you're like me, you might have wondered why your children can't understand you or can't empathize with you. Perhaps your children just need more time talking with you face-to-face, learning to mirror your feelings. But that kind of connection is easier said than done, isn't it?

All through life there seem to be things that pull parents and children apart. Work and school often separate us during the day. Our kids connect with teachers and coaches, and they find it especially easy to connect with friends. And even when we are with our kids physically—by being in each other's presence—we often don't connect emotionally. Because of this, small conflicts turn into big confrontations, which lead to anger. That's why finding a way to connect with our kids is so important. The more we connect and understand our kids, the more we feel what they're feeling and understand what they're going through. And the more they do the same when they connect with us.

Relationship over Rules

When we focus on the relationship over rules, we provide a positive interaction with our kids, building up the bond between parent and child. Focusing on the relationships closest to us is what God had in mind in the first place. In Mark 12:30–31 we read, "'Love the Lord your God with all your heart and with all your soul and with all your mind and with all your strength.' [And] 'Love your neighbor as yourself.' There is no commandment greater than these."

My friend and fellow author Amy Lively shed light on this word *neighbor* for me: "Jesus defined *neighbor* as anyone and everyone—regardless of their nationality or religion—with whom we live or whom we have the chance to meet. The Vulgate, a Latin translation of the Bible, uses the word *proximus* for neighbor. It means 'the nearest person or thing.' It shares the same root as *proximity* and *approximate*."[3] Reading Amy's words prompted a big revelation, since 90 percent of the day those in closest proximity to me are my kids. When I treat my children as I want to be treated—with tenderness, care, attention, love, and forgiveness—I'm not only following Jesus' command; I am giving my kids exactly what they need from me. As we build a connection, they are more patient with me and I am more patient with them. We are more empathetic with each other. They act out less, and I'm more gentle and caring when conflict arises.

Let's look at some of the specific ways we can foster connection and strengthen our relationships with our kids.

Giving Our Children Our Positive Attention

One of the scenes in the movie *The Sound of Music* shows Maria on a mountaintop, enjoying a picnic with the von Trapp children. She asks them why they were so mean to the previous governesses, and one of the children responds, "How else can we get Father's attention?"[4]

I don't know about you, but I find those words convicting. How many times have we been so busy that we didn't truly interact with our children until they acted out? Too many to count, right? So much of my day is spent managing my children—what they wear, what they eat, how they act—that sometimes I forget to give them the attention and connection they need.

When Buddy was almost three years old and having major behavior and anger problems, his therapist gave me an assignment:

have special one-on-one time with him. My "job" was to spend five minutes a day with Buddy, just the two of us, with no one else around. I was to offer a select variety of toys for him to play with and then let him choose what we played with. Then, once he chose, I was to follow his lead and do three things:

- Notice what he was doing and state it: "You have the red car."
- Repeat what he said: "Da car go fast." "Yes, the car goes fast."
- Praise him: "Great job lining up the cars" or "You are so kind to share with Mama."

Over and over again I was to do those three things. I was in no way to lead the conversation or direct the play.

As I look back on what happened during those one-on-one times, three things stand out. First, my son got exactly what he craved—quality time with me. Second, he felt seen, heard, and appreciated. Third, our one-on-one time together strengthened our relationship. I grew closer to my son, and he grew closer to me. After a few weeks of doing this, I noticed he was acting out less. He didn't seek my negative attention because he was getting my positive attention ... and it took only five minutes a day. (Frankly, we were usually having so much fun that it lasted longer.)

Even our older kids behave better when they feel they are getting some focused attention from me. As Gary Chapman, the author of *The 5 Love Languages of Teenagers*, pointed out: "If the teenager feels loved, then he has a much better opportunity of learning how to handle anger in a positive way. However, if the teenager's love tank is empty, the teenager will almost certainly handle anger poorly."[5]

A few months ago, one of my teen daughters had a meltdown at youth group. I'd jumped on her earlier that day because she was sitting on the couch with her electronic tablet instead of doing her chores. I raised my voice, and it triggered something inside her. Even after I apologized to her for yelling, she gave me the cold shoulder. I attempted to talk to my daughter a few times that day, but just when I thought she'd worked through her emotions, they'd flare up again, bigger and stronger each time.

By the time I was summoned out of my Bible study class to deal with my very upset daughter, she'd locked herself in one of the church bathrooms and was in emotional upheaval. She didn't want to talk to me, but she did want to talk to her dad, who was working out of town. The only way I could get her to let me into the bathroom was to put him on speakerphone.

John does a wonderful job of talking teen girls off emotional ledges, and I became the quiet phone holder who stood strong, even as she bad-mouthed me. My husband is masterful at reminding our kids to treat me with respect, even when they are mad, but getting my daughter to calm down and speak respectfully wasn't happening quickly.

After twenty minutes of talking on the phone and after my daughter had worked through all her emotions, she identified the true problem. She'd been feeling as if she wasn't being valued and heard. The fact was, I had been spending more time pointing out when she messed up than spending quality time with her, discovering what was in her mind and heart. My daughter wasn't feeling connected to me, and it showed.

At the end of the emotional day, within the locked church bathroom, my daughter and I made a plan to have fifteen minutes of "daughter-mom time" whenever she needed it. We made sure to have that special time the next day, and I assured her I was available for other days too. In a home with eleven people, creating one-on-one time is hard, but I've discovered that fifteen minutes of quality alone time helps my children feel loved.

Another way to fill our kids' "love tanks," one that requires no extra time commitment, is through positive words or praise.

Praising the Good, Ignoring the Bad

We parents can be quick to jump on our children when they are doing something we don't want them to do but slow to praise them when they are doing what they should be doing. The first time I learned the importance of over-the-top praising the good and ignoring the bad (emotionally speaking) was soon after we adopted our younger two children. As I've mentioned, not only did I send our kids to therapists, but I also attended therapy with them to learn how to parent angry children.

One thing the therapist told me to do was respond to a child's bad behavior in a monotone voice and with as little emotion as possible but to be exuberant in praise whenever that child did the slightest thing right. So if my daughter handed a cereal spoon to her sibling, I was to give her over-the-top praise for sharing. In the middle of a tantrum, when she paused her screaming to take a breath, I was to immediately jump in and praise my daughter for calming down (even though I knew she wasn't really calming down but simply trying to breathe).

I doubted this would work but agreed to try it. So whenever one of my kids acted out, I said something like "You need to make a better choice," being sure to keep any emotion out of my voice. Every time that child did something positive, I praised that child as loudly as I could, with as much enthusiasm as I could muster.

If my defiant three-year-old hurled a toy toward the toy box, I jumped up, clapped, and praised him for picking up his toys. As you might imagine, within seconds that toy actually did make it into the toy box. More than that, so did all the other toys. Not only did Buddy get excited about doing good things and receiving praise, but the two other little ones soon jumped in too, eager for the same response from me.

"Look at me, Mom!" one of my preschool girls would cry. "I'm helping too. Look at me!"

It took a conscious effort to ignore the bad and praise the good, but nothing has worked better in getting my kids to obey me. After the first day of my overexcited reactions, my husband returned home from work to a wife who had no voice left—and was very exhausted—but also to three children who were happy and excited about all the ways they'd obeyed that day.

Even though five years have passed since that time and even though I'm not as diligent as I should be, I've learned that this type of praise—when given with enthusiasm—still makes a huge impact in our home with all our children. With our older kids, the praise doesn't have to be as exuberant.

In fact, it's the daily moments when I catch our preteens or teens doing something good that matter most. When I notice them working hard on their homework, supporting a friend, or doing a chore without being asked, I tell them I appreciate their efforts. When I point out something I love about their character, personality, hobbies, or interests, that approval goes a long way. As an example, I've sat through conversations about comic books and makeup tips—praising a child's knowledge and wisdom—not because I was interested in those things but because my kids were. I wanted them to know I was proud they took time and effort to grow a passion or learn a skill.

Giving Kids What They Want

What fills your kids' love tanks? The two "love languages" we've talked about most in this chapter are one-on-one time and positive words and praise. Other "love languages" Gary Chapman identified in his popular book *The 5 Love Languages* are physical touch, receiving gifts, and acts of service.[6]

Even when it seems kids don't want it, they enjoy connecting with us through physical touch, like hugs, pats on the shoulder, or side-by-side snuggles on the couch. A few of my kids especially appreciate gifts. This doesn't mean they are selfish. It's just the way God created them. It simply means that when someone gives them a gift, they feel that person's love the most. They love it when I think of them and pick up small gifts for them, such as gum or stickers, when I go to the store. One of my daughters appreciates when I fold the clothes she left in the dryer (an act of service). Another lights up when I step in to help her with her chore. Still another gets excited when I offer to curl her hair for church. In each of these ways I'm serving my children beyond the cooking, cleaning, and carpooling that I do on a regular basis.

Still, what all kids want most is one thing: to spend time with Mom and Dad—real, quality, chill-out-and-have-fun-together time. Not only are children disappointed when they are merely shuffled from event to event; they're also physically and emotionally spent (which can also lead to anger issues, as we've mentioned). On the other hand, kids who have time to play, explore, create, and spend time with their families often don't have the same struggles with anger as other kids their ages. It's amazing, isn't it, that sometimes the best thing we can do to help our kids manage their anger is to just find ways to connect with them, in the ways that mean the most to them?

Reflection Questions

1. What are some ways your child lets you know he wants to feel more connected to you? How does spending one-on-one time with that child affect his anger issues?

2. Are you more prone to focus on rules or on relationship? Why? What happens when you focus more on the relationship than on the rules with your kids?

3. In what ways does loving your neighbor—loving your kids—reflect your love for God?

Action Steps

1. Plan a one-on-one playtime with one of your kids and do these three things. First, notice what he is doing and state it. Second, repeat what he says. Third, praise him. If possible, do this daily for a couple of weeks and note how your child's behavior changes.

2. List ways that each of your kids gets his love tank filled the most—time, words of praise, gifts, physical touch, or acts of service. Choose one thing to do with or for each child each day, no matter how small.

3. Sit down with your kids and talk about your schedule. Are there things that need to be cut to make time for family and creative connection? Cut them.

7

STOPPING THE CYCLE BEFORE IT STARTS

My six school-aged daughters and I were on an outing with other moms and daughters when six-year-old Aly decided to play in the sand. But it wasn't sand that she reached down to touch; it was hot ashes from a campfire. Immediately, her screams pierced the air.

I grabbed her, and with the help of one of the other moms, I began to tend to her wounds. We were trying to apply ointment and bandages when one of my older daughters, Maddie, rushed up and grabbed the ointment from my friend's hand.

"I need that. I burned my finger when we were making s'mores last night."

"Just a minute." I took the ointment back and winced as Aly screamed in my ear. "Your sister just burned herself really badly."

As soon as I took back the ointment, anger flashed in Maddie's eyes. She rose and raced away toward the cabin. My stomach sank as I realized she'd just been triggered. It turns out her little sister's injury had reminded her that she had burned herself the night before. It didn't matter to Maddie that I couldn't see a burn on her finger or that she hadn't mentioned the burn to me the previous night. My (to her ears) careless response opened a floodgate of pain and emotion in Maddie, more than I could have imagined.

As Maddie ran away, I watched her sister Grace join her … becoming part of the drama. While I still held a screaming child, Maddie ran to our cabin, grabbed her packed bags, and headed into the woods, attempting to run away. Grace was also mad at me for angering her sister, but Maddie's flight into the forest worried her more. She ran back to tell me what was happening.

I handed my six-year-old to my friend and went to find and calm my child who had just been triggered. I found her and tried to talk to her, but there was no getting through. Her emotions raged, and as she raced off again, I knew I had to get these kids home. One injured, two mad, and the others joining in with heightened emotions. Aly cried from the burn. Maddie and Grace cried with anger toward me. Sissy and Alexis cried because we had to cut the trip short, and Anna cried because her sisters were acting up again. I packed up the car as quickly as I could and got the crying and the angry girls in it. It wasn't a fun drive home.

I later realized that Aly's crying had triggered Maddie's feelings surrounding not being cared for in the past. These memories hit a core ache of rejection, which triggered her rage. And once rage erupted, there was no longer any connection between her emotions and rational thought. When I didn't tend to Maddie immediately, all the rejection she'd experienced during her early years, before we adopted her, came rushing back. She was running from the rejection and pain of the past. She was running to escape me, certain that our adoption would fail too.

My daughter's emotions caused her to run into the woods, even though logically it made no sense. (Where would she stay? How would she find shelter or food? What would happen when she got cold?) None of those rational things mattered in the height of her emotions. Once trigger thoughts launch angry kids into motion, it's hard to calm them down, let alone get them to think rationally.

This was not the only time one of my daughters has been triggered in this way. I'm thankful these kinds of angry emotions and irrational responses are mostly a thing of the past. How? By working with a therapist to train our kids to understand their trigger thoughts and stop their forward motion.

In this chapter, we'll explore what trigger thoughts are, and I'll share with you the tools that have been so helpful with our children.

What Are Trigger Thoughts?

There are two ways to understand triggers when it comes to dealing with our kids. The first type of trigger is the type we talked about in chapters 2 and 3. It's an external or internal stimulus that causes an angry reaction in our children. As we mentioned in those chapters, these triggers reflect how rested they are, their blood sugar levels, the events of the day, the trauma they have experienced, their chemical and hormonal balance, and more. If kids are tired or hungry, overstimulated or overwhelmed, they may have angry outbursts. According to Dr. Anita Bohensky, "Anger starts when a kid or teen feels in pain. The pain can be physical or emotional; it can be a stomachache or tiredness, feelings of being disliked or rejected; feeling that you are weak, foolish, ugly or many other kinds of pain."[1] There is a second type of trigger too. That is a *trigger thought* that goes off in the child's brain. A trigger thought isn't only about an external or internal stimulus. Instead, it's based on how a child *perceives* a situation. Something happens that causes pain, and the child directs the blame to another person. If a child can put the blame on someone else, it takes the attention off her own pain.

Here are some examples of trigger thoughts:

The coach called the wrong play; that's why I missed the shot. He's so stupid.

My mom doesn't care that I'm hurt. She never cares.

I don't have any friends. I'm always left out. People are so mean.

I'll never look like the girls on Instagram. All the guys think I'm ugly. I hate my mom for not letting me dye my hair.

These thoughts don't stay neutral. "[*Trigger thoughts*] are thoughts that blame other people or things for the painful feelings," wrote Bohensky. "When you get angry at something or someone else, *trigger thoughts* get rid of some of your immediate feelings of pain. But the problem is that having angry thoughts about someone else, while it can immediately get rid of some pain, it can also start a flood of angry and blaming thoughts that can go on and on."[2] Once a child is angry, it's easy for her to stay in an angry cycle—a cycle of thoughts, emotional upheavals, and physical responses.

The Cycle of Anger

The story at the beginning of this chapter perfectly illustrates the cycle of anger. Understand, all I described happened in just one minute.

To break it down, the cycle of anger looks like this.

1. *An event triggers your child's pain and anger.* It can be something another person says or does. It can be an unmet expectation. In my daughter's case, seeing her sister's pain reminded her of the pain of being burned the previous night, and she wanted to treat that pain. When I took the ointment back from her, in her mind I was telling her that she wasn't as important as her sister and I wasn't going to take care of her. This caused her to feel once again the emotional pain of the years of neglect she'd endured.

2. *The event, dialogue, or thought sparks trigger thoughts in your child's mind that focus the anger on another person.* With my daughter's emotional pain heightened, trigger thoughts filled her mind: *Mom doesn't care for me. She always treats me this way.* Additional thoughts flooded her brain: *I'm not wanted. This adoption is going to fail too. I need to leave. I can't go through the pain of abandonment again.*

3. *These trigger thoughts lead to a negative emotional response.* For my daughter, that response was fear, anger, and rage.

4. *As angry thoughts race and emotions rise, physical symptoms join in.* Maddie's face grew flush. Her heart pounded, her fists balled, and anger burned within her, and she could think of nothing else. These are all common reactions.

5. *Then a behavioral response occurs.* The trigger thoughts, emotions, and physical symptoms evoke a fight, flight, or freeze

response. At this point it's hard to talk with your child, who is too worked up to listen and too emotional to respond, except in anger. Once thoughts, emotions, and physical responses work together, anger is fully engaged.

When my daughter's trigger thoughts started her down the flight path, it was hard to get her to calm down so I could talk to her. My logical words couldn't break through to her later on the way home either. In fact, it took a few days before we could discuss what had happened and how we both responded. I was reminded again how impossible it is to try to be logical with children who have "flipped their lids."

Flipping One's Lid

Many people understand the phrase "flipping one's lid" as simply getting angry or flying off the handle, but I've discovered it has another meaning when applied to an out-of-control child. According to Dr. Daniel Siegel, "flipping one's lid" means a child's anger has caused the part of her brain that deals with emotions to disconnect from the part of her brain that deals with rational thought.[3] To put it in the simplest terms, anger has caused a disconnect of "wires" within the child's brain. In the moment of anger, nothing you say to calm your child will get through because of this disconnect. Anger blocks the logical words from getting through.

To better explain the concept of flipping one's lid, Dr. Siegel uses an example of a fist with a thumb tucked inside the fingers (see illustration).

FLIP THE LID (HAND MODEL OF THE BRAIN)

Make a **Fist** with your thumb tucked inside your fingers. This is a model of your brain.

Palm and Thumb = Stem and Limbic Area = Emotional Brain. This is where emotions and memories are processed. This is where fight, flight, or freeze is triggered.

Fingers = Cerebral Cortex = Rational Brain. Houses our ability to think and reason.

When something triggers us, we are prone to **"Flip our Lid"** which means the cortex (fingers) has a very poor connection with the limbic area (thumb), and we're not able to access the logical, problem-solving part of our brain. Our emotions are overriding our ability to think clearly.[4]

Unfortunately, it's usually in the midst of angry moments that we attempt to lecture our kids or teach them a lesson. But if our child has flipped her lid, rationalizations never work; the rational brain is no longer connected to the emotional brain, so neither common sense nor rational thinking will get through. In fact, trying to talk rationally with a child whose lid has flipped will only make things worse.

In addition, when a child flips her lid, all types of chemical reactions happen inside her body. "The adrenal glands flood the body with stress hormones, such as adrenaline and cortisol. The brain shunts blood away from the gut and towards the muscles, in preparation for physical exertion. Heart rate, blood pressure and respiration increase…. The mind is sharpened and focused,"[5] and the child's anger is truly all she can think about.

It's important to help kids understand what's happening inside their minds and bodies when negative thoughts get triggered so they don't get caught in the anger cycle—a cycle that can become a habit. "Acting out anger not only prolongs your angry feelings, it can make it easier to get angry the next time," wrote Dr. Anita Bohensky. "Not a good idea!"[6]

Have you ever felt that rush of angry emotions? I know I have. Has anger ever become a habit that's hard to break? I understand that too. As adults, gaining control of our emotions can be challenging, but it's even harder for kids. Self-regulation—the ability to calm ourselves—has a developmental aspect to it. The brain takes time to develop, which means that children don't have a fully developed frontal cortex—the part of the brain responsible for "emotional expression, problem solving, memory, language, judgment," inhibitory control (self-control), and other cognitive skills. "The frontal lobe is the 'control panel' of our personality and our ability to communicate."[7] The rational part of our children's brains won't be fully developed until they are twenty-five years old.[8]

That's why it's important to train our kids in how to respond to this flood of emotions and to their bodies' physical responses to anger. Our training can help them learn how to gain control.

How to Control Trigger Thoughts

So how can we help our children control their negative thoughts? By teaching them the three Cs:

1. Catch it: identify the thought that came *before* the emotion.

2. Check it: reflect on how accurate and useful the thought is.

3. Change it: change the thought to a more accurate or helpful one as needed.[9]

Catch It

When Maddie approached me to help with her burn, we each had our own story of what was happening. My story was that I had a badly burned younger child who needed my immediate attention, and since Maddie didn't have any evidence of burns and hadn't mentioned a burn the previous night—I felt she needed to wait.

Maddie's thoughts, however, reverted to a story she'd told herself since she was small: no one cared for her and people didn't help her when she was hurt. So when I didn't stop caring for her younger sister's burns to tend to her, my actions confirmed Maddie's beliefs. She told herself, *Mom must not care about me.*

With the guidance of our children's therapist, Maddie and our older adopted kids learned how to catch their trigger thoughts. Below are some of the things the therapist had them do. I share them here because they may give you some ideas about how you can help your own children with their trigger thoughts.

1. *Write a list of trigger words on a piece of paper and review them regularly with your child.* Explain to your child that if a thought contains one of these words, it is likely a thought that will trigger anger.

A few keywords in trigger thoughts are *should, shouldn't, must, must not, have to, ought to.*

He *ought to* share.

He *should* treat me better.

She *shouldn't* call me that name.

She *must not* care.

2. *Help your child "catch" other kinds of trigger thoughts by asking her after an anger episode what she was thinking about when she got mad.* Sometimes kids can figure out for themselves what their trigger thought was. Other times they will need adults to help connect the dots for them.

If your child is unable to identify her trigger thought, you can assist by saying something like "Do you want to know what I think? I've noticed that when you think I don't care about you, you get really angry with me and _____." You might be able to point out patterns that your child doesn't recognize. Usually there are a few specific things that make a child angry over and over again.

Here are a few examples of what I've said to our children to help them catch their trigger thoughts:

- "Whenever you and your sister start teasing each other, the words turn mean, and soon your words become hurtful toward each other. The teasing comments trigger the thought, *She shouldn't talk to me that way*, and then you get angry."
- "I've noticed that when you don't want to follow my directions, you stomp out of the room and start slamming things around. When I ask you to

do something, it triggers the thought, *She wants me to do too much. It's not fair.* Then you get really mad."

- "Whenever you don't think I've helped you with your homework, you slump to the ground, throw your pencil, and start crying and yelling. Being overwhelmed by your homework triggers the thoughts, *She doesn't care about me* and *I can't do this.* Then, in your anger, you have a meltdown."

Another way to identify trigger thoughts is to use emotions as cues. For example, if your child is experiencing a strong emotional reaction, ask, "Are you feeling anxious or depressed? How do you feel in your body right now? Is your heart beating fast? Look at your hands; are they balled into fists?" Then teach your child to pause and ask, "What thoughts are leading to these emotions? What pictures am I getting in my head?"

3. *Encourage your child to keep an anger log.* Anger often sneaks up and grabs control of our thoughts, emotions, and actions before we realize what's happening. With practice a child can get better at catching this anger before it takes over.

During my older children's therapy, the therapist often sent them home with worksheets they could use to record their thoughts and emotions. We put these sheets in a notebook for each of them and encouraged them to fill out the log whenever they got angry. These logs helped our kids gain awareness of what stirred anger in them; it also helped them identify patterns—such as recurring trigger thoughts that led to anger. Keeping a log helped them process not only what they felt but also the situation the caused their feelings.

An entry in an anger log might look something like this:

Date/Time	Saturday morning
Situation	Little brother knocked over the tower I built
Trigger Thoughts	He should leave my stuff alone
Strength of Feelings	Mad
Aggressive Behaviors	Threw blocks and yelled

As I mentioned, when your child logs her thoughts, feelings, and behaviors, it will reveal the patterns in her trigger thoughts. For example, one of our daughter's anger logs showed she was often getting into fights over colored pencils. The recurring thought that triggered the aggressive behavior was, *They should stop hogging all the pencils.* Or sometimes, *They should stop messing up the pencils I organized.* As we talked with her about this, together we came up with this solution: we purchased a box of colored pencils that was to be used only by her. She could control her own pencils and it solved a lot of angry interactions. This was a simple solution, and it came from recognizing trigger thoughts and looking for patterns.

Another time, all four of our teen girls were fighting in the bathroom as they prepared for bed. Their anger logs revealed they were all having recurring thoughts with a similar theme: *They should give me space. Everyone's shoving. I can't even get ready in peace!* These thoughts often culminated with the girls pushing and shoving one another and slamming doors. After noticing the pattern, we came up with an easy solution: only one girl in the bathroom at a time. As long as she wasn't dawdling or playing, the other girls couldn't pound on the door, try to get in, or complain. The fighting could have continued, with the same things triggering my daughters every day, but because we took time to figure out these things, we were able to devise ways to help our kids avoid being triggered.

Check It

Next, teach your child to check her thoughts. For example, when she is having an intense emotional response, encourage her to evaluate whether the trigger thought is true. Would Mom and Dad believe the same thing? If not, what would they think about it?

Examples of trigger thoughts include these:

My teacher doesn't like me. She never calls on me when I raise my hand.

My sister should let me wear those pants. I can't believe she won't share! I always let her borrow my clothes!

He ran into me on purpose.

Mom's going to blame me for breaking her glasses.

Some of these thoughts might have an element of truth. For example, another kid actually might have tried to trip your child on purpose. But most of these thoughts are just negative thoughts taken to an extreme.

You can help your children learn to check their thoughts by teaching them to ask themselves the following questions about their trigger thoughts. (We'll use the trigger thought *Mom's going to blame me for breaking her glasses* as an example of how a child might check this thought.)

1. What clues do I have about whether or not this thought is true? *My mom loves me. My mom will get mad that her glasses are broken, but when I calmly talk to her, she usually listens to me. These clues tell me the thought is not true.*
2. What should I do about it? *I should tell her I found her glasses and they are broken.*
3. What would I tell my friend to do if she were in the same situation? *I would tell my friend to go find her mom and tell her the truth.*

When a child learns to evaluate her thoughts in this way, she is better able to change them. Imagine how your child would handle situations differently if she learned to discover the truth behind her negative reactions and respond thoughtfully, not emotionally. All this centers on knowing and believing the truth.

Change It

The next step in the process, to change the thought, reminds me of Philippians 4:8: "Summing it all up, friends, I'd say you'll do best by filling your minds and meditating on things true, noble, reputable, authentic, compelling, gracious—the best, not the worst; the beautiful, not the ugly; things to praise, not things to curse" (THE MESSAGE). It takes a lot of practice, but parents can help angry kids learn to replace negative thoughts with ones that are positive and empowering. The key is to teach them to focus on *true thoughts*.

I've found two tools to be especially useful for helping kids replace their negative thoughts: thought notebooks and thinking cards.

Thought notebooks. One thought at a time, parents can teach kids to replace their negative thoughts and focus on positive thoughts instead. I do this by having our kids create a thought notebook in which they write negative (trigger) thoughts and positive thoughts side by side. I always encourage them to include a Scripture verse next to the positive thought to show that the positive one is rooted in God's Word.

For example:

NEGATIVE THOUGHTS	POSITIVE THOUGHTS
I am stupid.	*I am capable.* "For we are God's masterpiece. He has created us anew in Christ Jesus, so we can do the good things he planned for us long ago" (Eph. 2:10 NLT).
This is too hard. I can't do it.	*I can do this with help.* "God is our refuge and strength, always ready to help in times of trouble" (Ps. 46:1 NLT).
I should just give up.	*I will keep trying. I will not give up.* "But as for you, be strong and courageous, for your work will be rewarded." (2 Chron. 15:7 NLT).

When our kids focus on the truth of God's Word rather than on their negative thoughts, they find strength and guidance. It makes all the difference. Now that my kids have been using thought notebooks for a while, we don't see the same types of triggers and explosive anger we witnessed before. Part of the reason is that my children are more aware of their trigger thoughts and their patterns, but another large part of it is God's work in their lives.

Thinking cards. Thinking cards work especially well when a negative train of thought would have led to anger. I use them to teach our kids to think positively and choose wisely, instead of getting stuck on negative thoughts. Below are some examples of thinking cards my kids and I created to help them replace their negative thoughts about homework with positive, true thoughts.

NEGATIVE THOUGHTS	POSITIVE THOUGHTS
I don't want to do my homework now.	*I can work for ten minutes, and then I'll take a break.*
This is stupid homework.	*This will prepare me for my future.*
I'll never learn this.	*I've already learned a lot of things. I can figure this out.*
It's too much.	*I just have to do one step at a time.*
I'm dumb.	*What am I missing?*
I can't do math.	*I'm training my brain in math.*
It's good enough.	*Is this really my best work?*
I give up.	*That was plan A, my first try. What can I try next?*

Each of these negative/positive thought pairs can be written on an index card, with the negative thought on one side and the positive thought(s) on the other. When your children are in the midst of negative thought patterns, they can flip over the cards and read the positive thoughts.

Thinking cards can be created for anything that kids struggle with, things that usually lead to anger. They can be made for conflicts with siblings, chores, bedtime—you name it. My kids and I created the following card set for general thoughts:

NEGATIVE THOUGHTS	POSITIVE THOUGHTS
I can't do anything right.	*I may not get it right the first time, but I'm learning.*
It's too hard.	*I can do other things well, even if they are hard.*
I don't want to try.	*I'm getting better at trying things and succeeding at them.*
I give up.	*I'll try a new strategy. I'm learning.*
It will never get better.	*Things can get better. I'll keep trying.*
I messed up.	*I'll do better next time.*
That person is so much better than me.	*Each person has unique talents and gifts.*

Thinking cards can empower children to proactively make decisions and avoid getting stuck in a cycle of anger and frustration. When they start feeling discouraged, they can pull out a card and read through the positive side. Encourage your children to keep their cards in a spot where they can easily find them and to take them to school or anyplace where they may need to gain control of their thoughts, emotions, and actions.

When our kids learn how to catch, check, and change their trigger thoughts, they won't allow one negative thought to explode into a huge angry outburst. Instead, kids are better able to calm themselves. We'll talk more about how you can help them do that in the next chapter.

Reflection Questions

1. Why are trigger thoughts not about the current moment? What can they be about? What have they been about when it comes to your child's anger?

2. In what way can you tend to your child's wounds or needs in an effort to help calm trigger thoughts? Why is being aware of these wounds or needs important?

3. What trigger thoughts seem to set off your child the most? Make a list. Are these trigger thoughts similar to or different from your own?

Action Steps

1. Teach your child the three Cs concerning her thoughts: catch it, check it, change it. What does your child need to work on the most? What is a first step that you can help her take?

2. Help your child create an anger log. Record in it for a week. What patterns do you see? What simple changes can you make?

3. Help your child create a thought notebook or thinking cards and encourage her to write down her negative thoughts and then write down a positive thought to replace each one. Help your child find a Scripture verse that speaks truth confirming that positive thought and have her write it out next to the positive thought.

8

TEACHING KIDS TO CALM THEMSELVES

We were having a tough day at homeschool. I can't remember what triggered my daughter, but in the middle of our history lesson she flew off the handle at her sister. Within twenty seconds she rocketed from frustrated to angry. She jumped to her feet, threw down her book, and stormed out of the dining room.

"Please calm down—" I called after her.

"No! You never listen to me. I'm always the one who gets in trouble. You need to get *her* into trouble for once!"

"I will handle the situation with your sister, but I can't when you're acting this way."

My words had no impact on her behavior. She thundered up to her room. I took a deep breath. I wanted to make demands. I wished to give her a good lecture, but I knew neither would help. Anger rose within me, and I quickly sent up a prayer. Drawing another deep breath, I followed her up to her room.

The bedroom door was shut, and when I opened it, I found my daughter sprawled on her bed with a comforter over her head. Again, I held back my desire to lecture.

"You are angry," I stated simply.

"Yes, I'm angry."

I nodded and spoke in a low, firm voice. "You have ten minutes to calm yourself, and then come downstairs. We'll finish our schoolwork, and then we'll talk about how both you and your sister were acting."

I glanced at my watch, walked downstairs, and the rest of us continued our work. Ten minutes later, I heard footsteps approaching. I tensed, wondering whether the blowup would continue. Instead, my daughter sat in her seat without a word and continued her schoolwork. Later, she approached and apologized for the way she acted. I talked to both her and her sister about their actions. And I was reminded of something I'm learning: often the best way to calm kids is to allow them to calm themselves.

Perhaps you are thinking, *But, Tricia, didn't you say earlier that because their brains have not fully developed, children lack the cognitive skills to calm themselves when they are angry?* While this is true for younger children, kids can develop these skills as they grow older. My experience has demonstrated that with parental support and training, kids can come to understand their anger better and learn how to calm themselves.

Kids are smart. They are always learning new things. In the previous chapter, we talked about three resources they can use to understand their anger: an anger log, a thought notebook, and thinking cards. These resources can help children understand their reactions and thoughts so they don't get caught up in the cycle of anger. In this chapter, we'll look at how we can better use these tools to help our kids calm themselves, even if they've allowed anger to build and grow.

Understanding and Controlling the Mad

When children start to get mad, they view everything through the dark lens of their growing anger. Things that previously didn't bother them may seem humiliating or controlling. A simple comment may feel like criticism.

In our house, a child who is angry over homework may erupt with loud complaints, or he may start an argument when asked whether he did his chores. A child who got in an altercation with one sibling might lash out at a different brother or sister for something minor. I even saw a child getting mad over having to pass the salt because he was still worked up over a fight with a friend.

An angry child's thoughts may sound like this:

Mom ought to stop nagging me about chores. It just makes me mad.

He should just leave me alone. Everyone's ganging up on me.

Why do I have to be the one to help everyone? No one helps me.

Psych Central offers more examples of thoughts that continue to grow and turn into accusations, hate, and blame:

They did that on purpose.

They wanted to hurt me.

They deserve this.

They never even asked me.

They're being unreasonable.

They think you're better than me.

I'll show you.

It's not fair.

They started it.

They don't care about me.

They can't be trusted.[1]

Angry thoughts like these tend to spread and grow. Before kids know what's happening, they're in the middle of an explosive moment with a sister, shouting at a parent, or throwing things. Their accusations, hate, and blame have spun out of control. Yet there are things we can do to help our kids grow calm. We can teach them to:

- name and label their emotions,
- set limits on their behavior,
- come up with suitable compromises to their demands, and
- use proven tools to calm themselves.

Let's take a closer look at how each of these techniques can help our kids get on the pathway to calm.

Name and Label Their Emotions

One of the best things a parent can do for an angry child is to let him know you *are* paying attention and *are* aware of his emotions. When children are in an aroused state, they are often striving to get a point across. They sometimes use words, screams, or flailing. When we see our kids out of control like this, we often want to remove them from the situation. Or we may want to remove ourselves so we don't get angry too. So we send them to their rooms or put them in time-out. This usually doesn't help. Why? Because they are still not feeling "heard."

On the flip side, when a child knows you recognize his emotions and are paying attention, he feels heard. He doesn't need to escalate further to get his feelings across, because he can tell you are already tuning in. One of the best ways to help our kids feel heard—and to de-escalate the situation—is to label their emotions.

Douglas Noll, author of *De-escalate: How to Calm an Angry Person in 90 Seconds or Less*, teaches a technique called *affect labeling* that is extremely helpful to anyone attempting to calm another person, whether it be a parent calming a child, a teacher calming a student, or a prison guard calming a prisoner. "*Affect labeling* is the process of listening to another person's emotional experience and reflecting back those emotions in short, simple 'You' statements. A typical affect label would be: 'You are angry,'" wrote Noll.[2]

It really is as simple as it sounds. When you see your child in an emotional state, identify in one brief sentence the emotion he is feeling. Why does this work? Because so often as parents we demand our kids calm down without ever acknowledging their emotions in the first place. Either that, or we try to figure out *why* they are mad. As problem solvers, we want to figure out how this whole angry mess started, and then we want to get our children to stop the aggressive behavior as soon as possible. Or we're arguing with our kids over the actual words they're saying. We're trying to win an argument, prove a point, or threaten with consequences, while the child's emotions are simply screaming, "Pay attention to me!"

Noll explained that none of these common responses work, especially sparring with words. "Unlike with other forms of reflective listening," he wrote, "when you wish to calm someone down, you must ignore the words and pay attention to the emotions. This is counterintuitive to many people. We are trained to pay attention to words from the time we are born. Words communicate a lot of useful information. We are conditioned to speak, read, and listen to words. Because this skill is deeply engrained in us, we do not learn how to listen for emotions. Yes, we can recognize when someone is upset or angry, but we are not really listening to their emotions in a deep way."[3]

Children who aren't able to express their emotions lash out or hit something because they don't have the words to share what's going on inside. We give our children a gift if we *name and label their emotions*, allowing them to zero-in on their feelings. Noll stated that when we help a child, preteen, or teen by labeling his emotions, we're "loaning out our prefrontal cortex"—our reasoning skills—to him. And once the child is aware of what the emotion is, he often calms down quickly. Not only that, but we also build a connection by showing our children that we *are* paying attention.

Here are the three essential steps to affect labeling:

1. "Ignore the words being spoken.
2. Guess at the emotions [behind the words and actions].
3. Reflect the emotions with direct, declarative statements. (For example, 'You are angry, frustrated, and sad.')"[4]

As you work to label your child's emotions, both of you may be surprised by what's really going on. Noll explained, "There is no penalty for guessing wrong. Usually, if you label the wrong emotion, the speaker will correct you, saying, 'No, I'm not angry. I am frustrated!' In that case, you simply repeat the affect label by saying, 'Oh, you are frustrated.' I have never heard of or experienced someone becoming upset because the wrong emotion was labeled. People are so grateful that you are trying to really listen to them that they don't criticize your mistakes."[5] I've often found that what I thought was anger in my child was really anxiety. Or that what appeared to be rage was really fear. What are the basic emotions? Theorists disagree about the precise list, but in general the basic emotions at the core of emotional outbursts are anger, fear, anxiety, disgust, grief, shame/humiliation, abandonment, and feeling unloved.

Living in a home with girls, I deal with a lot of escalation. When I see one of my teens yelling at her sister, my conversation with her might go something like this:

"You are angry."

"Yes, I'm angry. She's always getting into my stuff."

"You are frustrated."

"Yes, because I already told her that if she needs something to just ask."

"You feel unloved."

"Yes, I wish she would just really think about me and not just herself."

My daughter then sighs and drops her shoulders as she relaxes and grows calm. She knows I'm paying attention to her, to her emotions. (Another benefit is that the offending sibling hears what her actions are doing to her sister. If this conversation is within earshot of the offender, I often turn to her and say, "You made your sister feel angry, frustrated, and unloved. Is that what you intended?" This helps our children see that their actions have deep, emotional consequences.)

This is a vastly different kind of conversation from those I used to have when my children fought. I used to try to figure out what they were arguing about, what stuff was gotten into, who took it, and how the conflict could be resolved. Those things can be worked out later, but the first step is to just get kids to move toward calm.

It's amazing how quickly affect labeling calms a child. Another benefit of affect labeling is that it teaches kids to recognize their own emotions. And once they have named their emotions, they can move on to the next step. "I am angry," a daughter will often tell me. "I am going to my room to calm down."

Set Limits on Their Behavior

While it is unrealistic to tell kids they can't get angry, that doesn't mean we shouldn't set limits for how they express their anger. For example, we can tell kids they are not allowed to hit or hurt people, destroy property, curse, or use harsh words. As a child works to stay within those limits, he is actually training himself to learn to become calm. How? Because he has to exercise some self-control in the midst of an angry moment to abide by your limits.

Parents can work together to decide the specific limits they want to set for their children. Once the list is made, it applies to everyone in the family. Yes, this means that all family members abide by the rules, parents included. The purpose is to help children know what is and isn't allowed and to practice self-control.

Once everyone agrees to the list of limits, it's helpful if each family member personalizes them. Each person capable of doing so can write them out. For example:

- Even if I'm angry, I will not throw things.
- Even if I'm angry, I will not destroy things.
- Even if I'm angry, I will not use my words to hurt people.

From there parents can work with children to brainstorm ideas for what not to do and what to do in order to calm down when they are angry. Here are more examples from our home:

- What not to do when angry: stomp, roll eyes, say "Whatever," argue, try to get a sibling to join my side.
- What to do to help me when I'm angry: go to my room to calm down, step away from the conflict, ask a parent for a few minutes of peace, ask a parent for help, pray.

When parents set limits on a child's angry behavior and when that child has identified some ways to calm down in the midst of feeling angry, it is easier for him to step away from the conflict and move toward calm. When my daughter grew angry with her sister—and then angry with me—she fled to her room because she'd discovered over time that's where she can calm down best. For her, staying in the middle of the drama—or staying too close to the person she's in conflict with—just keeps her worked up. In this case, retreating to her room was the right choice.

Make Suitable Compromises

When a child is angry because he's not getting what he wants, at some point he must decide what to do next. Will he continue to be angry, or can he find a compromise that will enable him to calm himself? Of course, finding a suitable compromise can be hard, especially when emotions are rising. Why? To discover a compromise, your child must think beyond the present moment. He must put aside that moment's emotions and instead think of an alternative, something other than what he wants.

Just as we can train our children to recognize their emotions and abide by set limits, we can train them to come up with compromises and thereby calm their anger. For example, let's say I'm cooking dinner and my young son comes in and asks me for a cookie. I don't want him to have one, because I know it would mean he won't eat the food I'm preparing. The conversation might go something like this:

"Can I have a cookie?"

"No, dinner's almost ready."

"I'm hungry!" he screams and slumps to the floor in anger.

There are a few things I can do. I can make him leave the kitchen. I could demand he change his attitude, but most kids don't know how to do this. Or I can help come up with a compromise that allows his need to be validated but in a more appropriate way. In this case I could say, "You can have a cookie after dinner." This compromise assures my son that I understand and that he will get what he is asking for, just at a different time.

When we make suitable compromises with our children, over time they learn to come up with their own solutions instead of just getting mad. Maybe they will ask, "Can I have a cookie after dinner?" or maybe they will choose to walk away and find a way to calm themselves.

When parents say things like "I know how you feel. It's frustrating, especially when our stomachs are hungry. Sometimes I want to have a cookie before dinner too," we show our children we understand their emotions, we care, and they are not alone in the way they feel.

In addition to naming and labeling their emotions, setting limits, and suggesting compromises, we can help our kids control their anger by teaching them tools they can use to calm themselves.

Use Proven Tools to Calm Themselves

Watch for Body Cues

The first step to helping kids know how to calm themselves is to teach them to understand what to watch for when they become angry. Anger causes physical things to happen in our bodies. As children's anger rises, their bodies respond in specific ways. Examples include shaking hands, breathing more quickly or heavily, raising their voices, desiring to scream, wanting to hit something, pacing, narrowing their gazes, clenching fists, tightening muscles, feeling hot, desiring to escape, faces heating up and turning red, feeling sick to their stomachs, experiencing aggressiveness, longing to cry.

Knowing these body cues—in addition to understanding negative thought patterns—can sharpen your child's awareness of what's happening inside. Your child can then work to pause long enough to understand his emotions, recognize limits, and choose compromises or ways to calm himself, instead of getting mad. Together with your child, make a list of the body cues he has. Make your own list of the cues your body gives you and compare the two. As different as people are, they usually have very similar body cues when it comes to anger.

Once a child recognizes anger rising, he needs to know what to do about it. One of the best tools I've found for helping my kids find ways to calm themselves when angry is calming cards.

Create and Use Calming Cards

Calming cards remind children how to act and react. Just making these cards with our kids can provide a good start to helping them know how to think and how to cope in the middle of a situation that might trigger anger. Then when they do get angry, we can encourage them to use the cards and do the things that help calm their anger.

Here are examples of calming activities my kids and I have come up with. Feel free to make calming cards with ideas from this list, but also encourage your kids to think up ideas of their own.

- Take a time-out
- Blow invisible bubbles with my breaths
- Move my body
- Think of consequences—how bad I'll feel if I let anger take control
- Imagine a happy place
- Talk to someone about what is bothering me
- Run or jump
- Squeeze Play-Doh
- Talk to a trusted friend
- Breathe deeply and count to ten
- Take a walk around the block
- Draw a picture of one of my favorite things

Each child will discover different things that help him calm himself. One of my daughters takes a bath to calm down. Another loves to squeeze Play-Doh or a stress ball. Still another daughter listens to some of her favorite music. Ideas can be added to calming cards over time, building your child's emotional toolbox.

Use Imagination to Bring Calm

One of my daughter's therapists taught her to create a fun, fictional place that she could think of when she started getting angry. My daughter created an imaginary place she called Rainbow Cuckoo Land—a place filled with rainbows, unicorns, and treats. My daughter described the place in detail, including all her favorite things that she imagined there. She also painted a picture of this place and kept it in her room. When she grew upset, I'd encourage her to chill for a while and imagine she was in Rainbow Cuckoo Land. Soon my daughter started doing this herself without my prompting.

Older kids might not want to create an imaginative land, but they can do something similar by thinking of a favorite movie scene or a favorite meme. Why can using their imaginations help kids grow calm? Because it's not possible to focus on two things at once. Either your child can focus on an imaginative place, or he can focus on his anger. Focusing on being angry causes the anger to grow and take control, while focusing on a special place or movie scene allows time for anger to dissipate.

In the book *Hot Stuff to Help Kids Chill Out*, Dr. Jerry Wilde encourages children and teens to use their imaginations to work through a common problem. He tells them to close their eyes and picture a situation in which they often get mad, such as with a parent, friend, or teacher. He tells them,

> Pretend you are actually there in your mind. See all the things going on in that scene. Hear the sounds that would be around you and everything about the situation. Make it as real as possible.
>
> Next imagine the scene like it is as you get mad. Go ahead and let yourself get good and ticked off just like you would if it were real life. Let yourself feel angry for several seconds.
>
> Now, instead of being really, really mad … calm yourself down. Stay in that scene in your mind but keep working until you get yourself calmed down.

When you get to the point where you've gotten your temper under control, take a deep breath and open up your eyes…. Write down exactly what you thought to yourself to calm yourself down.[6]

Walking through this exercise—and handling their anger appropriately in their imaginations—can help children learn how to handle similar situations in real life.

To teach kids how to do this, here are the steps again for parents to guide them through:

1. Imagine a situation in which you often get mad. Pretend you are actually there in your mind.
2. See all the things going on in that scene. Hear the sounds that would be around you. Make it as real as possible.
3. Go ahead and let yourself get good and ticked off, just as you would if it were real life. Let yourself feel angry for several seconds.
4. Now, instead of being really, really mad … calm yourself down.

A parent can use this role-playing activity to help a child think through different triggering scenarios. As with all the tools in this book, this one needs to be taught when kids are not in an angry moment. The more children learn to think through how to calm themselves when anger is not involved, the more capable they will be of calming themselves when it is.

Pray and Memorize Scripture

I cannot end this chapter without the reminder that all of us—children included—have another tool to use: turning to God for help. As we saw in the last chapter, Scripture memory is a great tool to help children tame their thoughts and control their emotions. Prayer and Scripture can also help them grow calm in the midst of anger.

Do your kids know they can send up a quick prayer in any situation, asking Jesus to help? Do they know Scripture talks in numerous places about how to handle anger? It's our job to teach our kids to pray and to lead them in Scripture memory. And truly the best way to do that is simply to practice. So, when you find yourself growing angry, pause and pray. When you see your children are getting upset, pause and pray. Pray aloud and with faith and humility. "Lord, we need Your help to calm down. These emotions feel so powerful, but we know that You are even more powerful."

Psalm 119:11 provides a good reminder of the importance of Scripture memory: "I have hidden your word in my heart that I might not sin against you." If our children have memorized God's Word, it will be a go-to resource they can turn to, especially when we are not around. I've included a list of wonderful Scripture verses parents and children can memorize together in the resource section at the back of this book.

Don't Give Up

Our kids need our help if they are going to learn how to calm themselves. The more they understand themselves and their anger, the better able they'll be to stop it before it starts and to calm themselves when it erupts. Remember, it might take a while for your child to do things like affect labeling, setting limits, or coming up with compromises for himself. Learning something new takes time. So don't give up on any of the tools or practices in this book, even if you're not seeing behavioral changes right away. The brain changes first, often slowly, and only after that do habits change. It takes time for thought changes to transfer to behavior changes, but once these changes happen, our kids can learn to move away from anger and toward calm.

Reflection Questions

1. Why is it important for your children to feel as if their emotions are being heard? How can affect labeling help an out-of-control child grow calm?

2. What limits have you set around anger for yourself and your family? How can you help your child better understand those limits so he begins to learn self-control?

3. In what ways can prayer help a child with anger issues? How can you help your child understand prayer better?

Action Steps

1. Teach your child how to affect label another person. Watch videos or television shows and try to label what emotion the person is displaying. Teach your

child how to affect label a sibling who is escalated, instead of joining in the fight. Finally, encourage your child to affect label himself when he is getting angry.

2. Create a set of calming cards with your child and teach him how to use the cards. Applaud his efforts when he uses the cards to calm himself down.

3. Work with your child to use his imagination to help him when he is angry. If it's a younger child, help create an imaginary place he can think of when he's angry. If it's an older child, help him use his imagination to step through a common situation that makes him angry, but also help him calm down from that situation in his mind.

9

CALMING ANGRY BABIES, TODDLERS, AND PRESCHOOLERS

I set the orange plastic cup in front of my toddler. "No! Blue cup!" She scrunched her face and pushed it out of the way, nearly knocking it off the table. Later, the cup lay on its side, with juice running all over the table. Something had angered her. I wasn't quite sure what it was this time. In tears, she fell in a heap to the floor. The sticky mess on the table was bothersome enough, but even worse was the toddler in the midst of a fit. Why did dealing with an angry toddler have to be so challenging?

When I became a mom, I expected my children's anger to manifest itself more when they were school aged and didn't get their way. I thought angry fits would happen over bedtime or discipline. I didn't know how to handle my little ones when they got angry. I didn't expect toddlers to ball their fists and pound the floor in anger. Or that I'd have a baby who would furrow her brow and scream in rage.

Anger, it seems, emerges at any age. Babies and young children have needs and wants, and when these aren't fulfilled, they are sure to let you know. The problem arises when we don't know how to handle their anger. Or worse, when their anger triggers our own. I never imagined I could get so worked up over a toddler's fit. Thankfully, some great tools can help us distinguish our children's needs, understand them better, and handle their anger without losing our cool.

Anger and Babies

Babies cry because they need to be fed, held, or changed or because they're tired, sick, or in pain. Crying is the only way they can alert us that something is wrong. It's our job to figure out what they need.

Once a baby's need is met, the baby will stop crying … or not. Numerous times my babies got so frustrated trying to communicate a need that anger took over. Then, even after I changed the diaper or made a bottle, the crying continued simply because the baby was worked up. Once crying releases a baby's anger, she is usually able to settle down. Sometimes what a baby needs is to be comforted while she cries and then, after she has calmed down, to have her additional needs met for food, a clean diaper, or a nap.

Babies also cry when they sense we are angry and tense, because it makes them feel angry and tense. In this case, the best thing we can do is calm ourselves and then tend to our child.

It's important to realize that babies do not cry because they are stubborn or because they're having a tantrum. That doesn't happen until a child is twelve months to eighteen months old. So when a baby cries—even with an angry cry—it's because there is a legitimate need, and it's our job to meet that need in a loving way.

How we tend to and care for our babies—or don't—sets the foundation for how our kids will interact with people for the rest of their lives. Whether a caregiver responds to a baby with anger or love, neglect or care, empathy or lack of emotion, significantly affects how that baby's brain develops. It sets that child up for life. When a baby is nurtured, it helps her develop a larger hippocampus, the region of the brain important for learning, memory, and stress responses.

According to Live Science, "Brain images have now revealed that a mother's love physically affects the volume of her child's hippocampus. In the study, children of nurturing mothers had hippocampal volumes 10 percent larger than children whose mothers were not as nurturing. Research has suggested a link between a larger hippocampus and better memory."[1] More than that, as Dr. Karen DeBord wrote, "If a child is raised in a loving setting, they will learn to love."[2] "Caring physical contact also makes children feel secure. They are able to form caring relationships with others."[3]

In contrast, studies show that the brains of children who are ignored or neglected do not fully develop in all areas. According to Dana Suskind, author of *Thirty Million Words: Building a Child's Brain*, "Living in environments that are chronically 'blank faced' or, even worse, angry and hostile, is not something that, in a few seconds, will be rectified with a hug. In those cases ... stress hormones such as cortisol begin bathing the babies' brains, the profoundly negative, often irreversible, effects permeating their core. The result is observable not only in cognitive and linguistic development, but also in behavior, self-control, emotional stability, social development, and overall mental and physical health."[4]

In other words, a parent's loving and positive response helps build all the right connections in a child's brain. It provides stability in a child. It teaches her how to love, how to build bonds, and how to handle stress. All these things will help a child be better equipped to manage anger as she grows older.

Toddlers: Choosing the Wrong Hills to Die On

Things change as babies become toddlers. They start communicating in right and wrong ways. For some reason we often think toddlers should have complete control of their actions and emotions. Often we turn ordinary childhood issues into battles we feel we have to fight and win. We see childish, angry reactions and assume our toddler is simply being defiant when that's not the case at all.

I recently attended a training session for parents of children with feeding disorders, and the speaker, Janine Watson, was discussing picky eaters. She stated that 50 percent of all children ages eighteen months to twenty-four months are picky eaters. Picky eating is developmentally normal. Many new foods are introduced to children at this age. It's only normal that toddlers won't like some foods. It's also normal for young kids to want to eat only familiar foods.[5] Yet for some reason we parents often push the issue until our kids become angry. Then we label their reaction as a control issue or an obedience issue when it's not.

My oldest daughter was an especially picky eater. When she was little, she often pushed food around on her plate and refused to eat. She also didn't like her food to touch, and she would get angry if it did. At first John and I turned this into a battle, but then an older, wiser mom encouraged us not to pick that as a hill to die on. After that, we offered our daughter new foods, but we didn't force her to eat everything on her plate. Instead, we insisted she try everything—just one bite. We learned that going beyond that was not worth the fight. And the great part is our daughter is now grown and she eats well. She still is slightly picky, but it hasn't negatively affected her life.

Other issues not worth fighting about with toddlers include wearing mismatched clothes, wanting to eat the same things every day for lunch, or not keeping their toys picked up.

But health and safety issues are worth going to battle over. Toddlers simply shouldn't touch certain unsafe things. They should obey their parents, stay in safe areas, and not be allowed to roam. They should eat healthy food, even if it is monotonous. They should be taught not to hit or hurt others. These are things worth putting up a fight over.

One thing I often ask myself when dealing with a toddler is "How much will this matter five years from now?" Training our children to stay safe, obey, and care for others will matter. Clothing choices or whether our child eats peanut butter and jelly every day for weeks won't.

Understanding a Preschooler's Frustration

Many things frustrate children as they grow from toddlers to preschoolers. Often what we label as "bad behavior" is due to uncertainty, fear, overstimulation, physical exhaustion, or hunger. A lack of verbal skills—leaving children unable to communicate their thoughts or feelings—can also frustrate them and cause them to hit, bite, scream, or pout.

Preschoolers also may get angry because the world is new and exciting and they want to experience everything. They want to do all the things older kids and adults do (like cook or mow the yard), yet parents who know they don't have the ability to do those things and are just trying to keep them safe "hold them back."

Preschoolers may also become frustrated and angry when asked to do things they don't have the physical or mental skills to do or when a lot is expected of them, such as eating without making a mess or drinking from a cup without spilling or having to sit quietly for longer than a few minutes. Yet so many times we expect just these things of them.

Preschoolers are quick to learn that angry outbursts make them feel powerful and that they get attention by hitting, biting, screaming, or pouting. Anger is the one emotion they know to display well, and they use it often.

Getting Ahead of a Young Child's Anger

Our young children's anger shouldn't surprise us. Instead, we should be prepared. Wise parents are not only ready for outbursts; they also know what pushes their preschoolers' anger buttons and figure out ways to keep their children's anger from being triggered.

Here are some things you can do to help prevent outbursts.

1. *Prepare your child, as well as you can, for situations that might make her angry.* Talk with her in advance about the things or situations that make her angry. For example, if you know your preschooler gets mad about having to share toys—and she will soon have to do this—you might prepare her by saying something like this: "Your friend is coming over. He will want to play with your toys. Are there any toys you don't want him to play with? Let's put your favorite toys away and pick out a few toys you'll be happy to share."

2. *Think ahead and make challenging situations as easy as possible for your child.* If your child will be going to a new Sunday school class soon, take her to meet the teacher, then sit together, watch the class for a while, and talk about what the kids are doing.

3. *Give your preschooler time and space to get her energy out.* Don't expect a preschooler to be quiet and sit still for a long period of time. But for times when she does need to sit still and be (relatively) quiet, consider making a "quiet bag." Put some small coloring books, crayons, or small toys into the bag so your child can entertain herself when she needs to be quiet. Snacks are always helpful too. Planning ahead can save a lot of grief. Also be sure to praise your preschooler for a job well done when she does sit quietly.

4. *Recognize the difference between a preschooler's childish and willful behaviors.* Childish behaviors are things kids do because they don't know better, lack necessary coordination, or don't understand their actions. For example, when a very young child sets down a cup at the table's edge, causing it to spill, the behavior is childish, not willful or defiant. She doesn't know any better and is still learning how to maneuver her arms, hands, and cups in the space around her.

On the other hand, if your child looked at you, narrowed her gaze, and then purposefully tipped over a cup, that behavior would be willful and defiant.

If she knocks the cup over because of childish behavior, you might want to teach your child how to put a cup on the table so it isn't likely to get knocked over the edge. Or you may just continue to use a cup with a lid for a while. If she knocks over the cup because of willful behavior, you might want to enforce a consequence for the behavior.

Is there anger behind your child's actions? Willful acts are often a normal part of a preschooler testing limits. If there is anger, it can be addressed by saying something like, "You are angry. Let's think of another way to handle our anger." One way our therapist taught our younger kids to calm themselves was teaching them to "fold their hands, take a deep breath, and pray" when they are angry. This works amazingly well, even for small kids.

5. *Set simple expectations and rules so your preschooler can succeed.* We shouldn't expect our preschoolers to make huge changes overnight. That's why it's important to have a few simple rules. For example, John and I didn't expect our preschoolers to have perfect table manners, but neither did we let them run and play during mealtimes. We had a rule that they had to sit with us while we ate (and while they sort of ate). We used good manners to teach good manners, and we remained consistent in what we expected of our kids. We also had simple rules such as "no biting" or "no hitting." As our children got used to our expectations and adopted good manners, our preschoolers experienced fewer angry outbursts.

Also, even if you can't avoid every episode that may upset your child and although you can't make everything better, you can empathize. You can say things like, "I know you don't like people looking at you in the store. Sometimes Mommy doesn't like people looking at me either."

What expectations and rules have you set for your child? Make a short list and focus on one thing at a time. Maybe you can work on no biting and no hitting and then tackle sitting at the table during mealtimes. Yes, it's important to have children who are loving, respectful, and well behaved, but our goal is to *teach* them what this means, day-by-day.

The one thing you can count on with young children is unpredictability. While you can do your best to plan, expect the unexpected. Preschoolers are on a quest for independence, and small frustrations can transform into big angry outbursts. They will test limits, and they don't understand consequences. But as they grow and mature, their understanding will grow too.

Teaching Young Children about Emotions

One of our jobs as parents is to help our kids understand their feelings and learn how they can respond appropriately, and this training begins when they are toddlers and preschoolers. The importance of labeling emotions was discussed in chapter 8, but I want to return to it here because even preschoolers can be taught how to label their feelings, including anger.

According to Daniel J. Siegel and Tina Payne Bryson, authors of *The Whole-Brain Child*,

> In terms of development, very young children are right-hemisphere dominant, especially during their first three years. They haven't mastered the ability to use logic and words to express their feelings, and they live their lives completely in the moment— which is why they will drop everything to squat down and fully absorb themselves in watching a ladybug crawl along the sidewalk, not caring one bit that they are late for their toddler music class. Logic, responsibilities, and time don't exist for them yet. But when a toddler begins asking "Why?" all the time, you know that the left brain is beginning to really kick in.[6]

Since children under the age of four don't have the ability to use logic and words to express their feelings, they often respond in anger even when they are experiencing a different emotion.

One of our daughters moved into our home at five years old. She also had no idea how to express what she felt or how to label what was happening inside her. When she got physically hurt, she became angry, and she screamed or hit the wall. When she was frustrated, she kicked and screamed, pushing me away when I tried to help her. Sometimes when something really good was happening, she got angry then too. She actually sabotaged joyful moments because she didn't know how to handle her emotions.

When I discussed this with her therapist, she explained, "You don't know how emotions were presented or taught during her early years. When she was hurt, she could have been laughed at. Or she could have been spanked because she was bothering someone with her crying. Maybe her anger stems from feeling the pain, being afraid, and being unsure what to do about the pain."

This was eye opening to me. After learning that, I worked to teach my daughter about emotions and how to label them. When she was angry, I labeled it.

For example, when her brother took her toy, I told her, "You are angry."

When she was sad, I labeled that too. "I know you wanted to go to the store, but we are not going today. You are disappointed and sad."

When she was physically hurt, I extended my arms. "You're hurt. Come to Mommy. Mommy will give you a hug, hold you, and I'll do what I can to help you feel better."

Slowly, day-by-day, emotion-by-emotion, my daughter started to understand her emotions and how to deal with them. When she was angry, she learned to allow me to help her calm down instead of pushing me away and having her anger grow into rage. When she was sad, she learned it was okay to be disappointed and sometimes when we're sad, we need a hug too. And when she was hurt, she learned to seek me out for comfort. I clearly remember the day when everything changed. After I'd told her dozens of times to come to Mama when she was hurt, she finally did. It brought me so much joy in that moment to know she'd learned to trust me. I was a safe haven for her emotions.

Of course, right away we discovered we needed to teach our daughter that there were other safe people she could trust too. Once, John was outside playing with the kids and I was inside cooking dinner when my daughter fell off her bike and hurt herself. Immediately she stood and started rushing toward the door into the house, which was near where John stood. He knelt down and opened his arms, but instead of running to him, she ran inside to me. "Mommy, Mommy!" she cried. I had taught my daughter to come to *me* when she was hurt. I'd failed to teach her that she could go to her daddy for comfort too. After that, we started teaching her there were other safe people she could trust too.

In addition to teaching kids the importance of understanding their emotions, it's also vital to teach them how to use their words, instead of simply acting out when they grow angry.

Teaching Kids to Use Their Words

"Children between two and seven years of age often chat away, no one else in sight," wrote Dana Suskind. "It turns out that a key mental tool in children's self-regulation is talking to themselves. Private speech among preschool children, also known as 'self-talk,' is actually predictive of greater social skills and fewer behavioral problems. Teachers rated these children higher for self-regulation."[7] So whether a young child is talking to others or simply talking to herself, the act is helping her understand how to interact with the world around her.

Suskind also said that storytelling can help a preschooler understand her feelings. For a preschooler, storytelling means trying to tell about an event and sharing her thoughts and emotions about that event in the best way she knows how. For example, if your child is injured on a slide, she might be afraid to go down the slide again. You might even make her angry if you try to force her to do so. But at the same time, she might want to talk about what happened over and over. A preschooler may say something like this: "The slide is too big. I fell off. I hate that slide. That slide made me angry." She might repeat the same story over and over, to you and to others. Your preschooler is expressing her emotions in the way she knows how.

Storytelling works for any experience that stirs up fear or anger. It helps a child grasp her feelings about what happened. The more she's able to put words to her experience, the more she can understand what's going on inside. Make it your habit to say "Use your words" anytime anger escalates into tantrums or rage. "Doing this consistently and appropriately will help a child learn how to understand, identify, and express emotions and even to develop better self-regulation," wrote Suskind.[8] In fact, anytime you can explain a situation to a child in your own words, it helps. It's a model for your kids too.

Being Proactive to Prevent Misbehavior

Preschoolers learn a lot about their own actions by our reactions to them. Have you ever noticed a preschooler looking at you when she's reaching for something she's not supposed to touch? She wants to know—by your reaction—how serious you are. She wants to know her limits, and she tests those limits by pushing them. Sometimes it seems that getting angry is the only way we can get our preschoolers' attention, yet this often leads to them waiting for us to get angry before they obey. Not a good habit to develop. We need our preschoolers to obey anytime we give them a directive, not just when we're angry.

Instead of reacting to misbehavior, we can be proactive and teach preschoolers how to behave in certain situations. One of the ways we can do this is by role-playing new situations. For example, take your child's small hand and walk her through an act of obedience, such as putting her toys back in the toy box when she is done playing. If your child knows what you expect her to do, she won't get angry trying to figure it out.

Yet as much as we'd like to be able to, we won't be able to prepare our children for everything. The key is letting our children know that hard stuff will come and it's okay to have various emotions. As Siegel and Bryson wrote, "Rather than trying to shelter our children from life's inevitable difficulties, we can help them integrate those experiences into their understanding of the world and learn from them. How our kids make sense of their young lives is not only about what happens to them but also about how their parents, teachers, and other caregivers respond."[9] I intentionally have tried to show our kids through my behavior that God is there and wants to help us. I do this by praying in their presence for situations I face. I also do this by helping my preschooler pray for the situations in her life. I want her to know she can turn to God when she is sad or scared or angry.

Nurturing Preschoolers' Spiritual Side

My friend Francie often reminds me that it's never too early to teach children about spiritual things. She's encouraged me to see my children from a kingdom perspective so when they explode in anger, I can remind them who God says they are.

Francie often sits with her little ones on her lap and speaks God's truths over them: "You are loved by God. He has great plans for your life." She also asks the Lord to show her His purposes for her children—their unique strengths and weaknesses. It's something I'm learning to do too.

"One of our children we call Powerful Heart," Francie said. "She loves big, and she expresses big on opposite sides of the spectrum. Instead of just complaining, 'Why are you so dramatic and intense?' when she gets angry, I say, 'Okay, little lovey. God wants to give you His Spirit, and His Spirit includes self-control, so we're going to take a minute, and we're going to breathe. Next time you feel this anger, I want you to ask me to help you, and we're going to ask the Spirit to help you, because He's given you a spirit of power and love and self-control. Not a spirit of rage, but a spirit of peace.'"

I love how Francie is teaching her little ones to come to her for help. When they do, she prays with them and together they seek help from God.

I too love praying with my children. When I see them growing angry, I often say, "Let's take a minute and pray about that. Do you want me to start?" They rarely refuse. My young children are thankful and relieved when I help them turn to God for strength, self-control, and help. It shows them that I am there to help and God is too. And as my children have grown older, they've also developed a habit of turning to God in prayer.

Filling Your Home with Love and Healing

Last, it's important to fill our homes with love and healing. When young kids are allowed to make anger a habit, it perpetuates an unhealthy environment for all involved.

"When my kids get angry, I encourage slow deep breaths, prayer, soft eyes, and hymns," my friend Tamara said while encouraging me one day when I was feeling overwhelmed by my kids' emotions. "The more stress in the home or the more I feel my kids ramping up, I play calmer worship," she added. I've followed Tamara's lead, and I've discovered that when I put on worshipful music, calm myself, and focus on God—and help my kids do the same—it makes a huge difference.

"I realize how much I set the tone for my home, especially when I'm operating from a place of worship," added Francie. "When my heart is settled and filled, I can experience my kids' tantrums with a lot more peace and I can lead them back to the calm waters. But when I'm not settled, then I also act like a three-year-old. They blow up, and then I blow up. Much better is welcoming God all day as our honored, welcomed guest."

I've also learned to be aware of what comes into my home through the media—are the messages peaceful or full of strife? The airwaves are filled with ways the Enemy is trying to discourage us. The media often sows seeds of anxiety, fear, and frustration. I see a noticeable difference when I enter my day with a settled heart and a settled home.

When parents create a home of love and healing, it provides a safe place for babies, toddlers, and preschoolers to learn about their emotions and how to interact with the world. The more caring, helpful, and understanding we make ourselves and our environments, the better our children will respond—not just today but for days to come.

Reflection Questions

1. In what ways can your love, care, and training about emotions help your child learn to self-regulate?
2. How does listening to our children's stories about hard or emotional situations help them process their experiences? In what ways can you become a better listener?
3. How can your hugs, your words, and God's truth help children see who they really are, even if they struggle with anger?

Action Steps

1. Make a list of ways you'd like to train your young child concerning her emotions, actions, and reactions. Also make a list of things you've decided are not hills worth dying on. Choose one thing to focus on first. What's a first step toward it?

2. Create a list of situations in which your child struggles with anger. For each situation, write one or two things that can help you prepare your child for that situation. How can you set up your child to succeed?

3. Make a list of things you can do to make your home a place of love and healing. What can you do to help your heart find peace in your day so you can better help your young kids?

10

CALMING PRETEEN ANGER

I paused a few paces into the bedroom, unable to take another step without walking on clothes, hangers, books, papers, and random girlish things. My daughter looked up from her tablet.

I glanced around, sighed, yet kept my voice soft. "Hmm, you haven't touched this room and you're on electronics? Let me hold that for you until you're done."

"No. That's not fair! I was just listening to music."

As if I believe that.

"You have a CD player for music. Your electronics are turning into a distraction."

My daughter rolled her eyes—a gesture preteens have perfected over generations, I'm sure.

I took her tablet and said, "If you just focus on cleaning, I'm sure it'll only take you thirty minutes—"

She picked up a book and threw it toward the bookshelf. "I know, Mom."

"Thirty minutes," I repeated as I exited the room. "I'll come back and check."

"Whatever …" *Wham!* Another book hit the bookshelf, and I resisted the urge to turn and give a lecture. The words were on my lips, but I knew they would do no good. My heart pounded. If I have a trigger word, it is *whatever,* but I refused to allow my emotions to get engaged. She wasn't going to pull me into this fight, I decided.

As a mom with kids of all ages, the hardest age for me is preteens. Why did I jump straight to the preteens when talking about ages and stages? Babies, toddlers, preschoolers, and preteens are times of huge developmental transitions. All the basic techniques I taught earlier in the book work well with elementary school-aged children, but I wanted to go into further detail when it comes to these huge life transitions. And believe me, when it comes to preteens, there are huge developmental transitions.

Children who are ten, eleven, and twelve years old are part child and part teenager. There are early signs of puberty during these years, and hormone changes often make preteens irritable. At this age kids strive to become more independent and test authority, especially their parents'. This often leads to them being mouthy. Preteens not only know how to use their words "well"; they also know how to push their parents' buttons.

Preteens seem to fly off the handle at every little thing. If an angry preteen has held in frustrated feelings for a long time, he is ready to be heard—and may even become aggressive and physical. Preteens can feel isolated and frightened by all the changes within themselves, their friends, and their peers, and these feelings come out through anger. Preteens often release anger in a safe place— with you.

The hormones raging within preteens make settling down difficult for them. The emotions surging through them feel *very* real. And because preteens excel at upsetting parents, we may not be as willing to try to help our preteen calm down. Why should we help with the way he is acting? Or maybe we don't know how to help. We're at a loss to unravel the tangled mess of emotions inside our kid. When the anger erupts, we can't just send a preteen to bed early or put him in time-out. Instead, one of the best things we can do with an angry preteen is not get drawn into our child's frustrated and angry emotions.

When my daughter got angry because I asked her to clean up her messy room, I knew she was trying to pull me into her anger. When I didn't join in, she quickly calmed herself and got busy obeying me. When I returned to her room thirty minutes later, she was proud of her efforts. In essence, I helped calm my daughter by not giving her an avenue for her anger to increase in the first place. I did it by reminding her of what was required, removing distractions, giving her a time limit (so the drama wouldn't continue all night), and not getting drawn into the fight. Sometimes the best way to calm preteens is to do the opposite of what our own emotions tell us to do.

Loosening the Reins

The preteen years bring big changes for parents too. We are used to directing our kids' every move. Sometimes it's hard to give them space to make their own decisions, but if we don't, preteens are likely to feel that we don't trust them and we still want all the control. (Which may be true.) During the preteen years, parents have to loosen the reins on attempting to control their children's behavior. Here are a few ways to do just that.

1. *Avoid power struggles.* This is true throughout the parent-child relationship; it's just that the battlegrounds change as a child gets older. But no matter a child's age, when it comes to a struggle of the wills, we can ask ourselves, "How much will this really matter in the long run?" I've learned not to care as much about things that won't really matter in the long run—like my preteen daughter wearing the same shirt three days in a row (as long as she doesn't stink)—and to focus instead on her attitude and the concerns of her heart. For most things I offer my preteen choices, such as what she wants in her lunch or when she wants to do her homework—before or after dinner. But she also knows I have a list of nonnegotiable things. She must shower daily. She must do her chores. When preteens know what things *must* be done, they are far less likely to fight about them.

2. *Let him be moody.* Preteens will be moody. It's a given. I just ask our preteens to take their moodiness with them to another room. While it never works to demand that they change their moodiness, if I give them time and space to be moody, their emotions eventually level out. It usually takes an hour for my kids to come around. If it takes longer than that, I know a bigger issue is happening in my child's heart, and I set aside some time to talk with my preteen.

3. *Make time to communicate with your preteen.* That's *make* time not *take* time. Preteens want to know we care about what they care about. I've found that the best time to talk with my preteens and teens is when it's their idea. These moments often become the best relationship-building times with my kids. Sometimes they come late at night, and I have to make myself stay awake to be present with them. But when I make

time for them, my preteens feel heard, and in return they develop more respect and appreciation for me, which leads to fewer angry episodes.

I've also found it helps to plan things to do with my preteens, to simply hang out together. Sometimes we talk about their struggles, but often we don't. I chat with my kids about all types of things. "Talking about abstract things is important," wrote Tom Burns. "Having big, wild conversations about concepts like art, music, time travel, and dreams makes it much easier when you'll eventually need to talk about things like anger, sadness, pain, and love."[1] I love knowing that we don't have to talk about the crisis of the moment, that our kids actually need us to talk with them about other, seemingly unimportant stuff.

4. *Allow your kid to experience consequences.* Is your preteen moody and angry about having to study for a test? Let him decide how much he will study. But also let him know he'll have to deal with the consequences of a bad grade. The only way preteens will learn to make good decisions is if we allow them to try and fail and to try and succeed.

"If we never let our kids struggle to get something they want or work through a problem for themselves, then when things get difficult later in life," explained Foster Cline and Jim Fay, "they won't suddenly turn tough and get going; instead, they'll just quit."[2] Sometimes the best way to help your child is just to step back and let your kid make his own decisions, even if it means he doesn't like the consequences or the consequences make him angry. Hopefully, with our guidance, preteens will start to understand that they can make things easier on themselves by making better choices.

5. *Be empathetic.* Remember how hard and confusing things were when you were a preteen? Thinking back may help you be more

understanding. Also, consider how much more challenging things are for your child now that he is in middle school. Middle schoolers go through a lot of changes. They now have multiple teachers instead of just one, and those teachers may have different expectations. They have to figure out how to manage their time so they can get from one classroom to the next without being late. On top of that, many preteens face a lot of social pressure. Both boys and girls worry about fitting in and making friends. Many preteens deal with cliques, bullies, and feeling left out.

You can help your middle schooler avoid getting overwhelmed and angry by talking through these changes and helping him organize his schedule and daily routines. It's a good time for your child to learn how to break big projects into small chunks.

100 Percent True, Not Necessarily 100 Percent Right

We can also help our preteens be calmer by teaching them that even if they feel things—or believe things—it doesn't mean their emotions, interpretations, and perceptions are spot on.

Anger simmered in my kids' eyes as they sat around the table. We'd been through several days of hard feelings, miscommunication, and tense emotions. It seemed as if everything I tried to do for them blew up in my face. It was time for a family meeting.

I sat down with my kids and looked around the table, meeting each child eye-to-eye. Then I said, "There is something we need to talk about. There have been a lot of emotions lately, and I know they feel real … but let's talk about whether they're accurate. Sometimes I can't give you my immediate attention. Sometimes I need to say no to one of your requests. There have been times when you thought I'd given you a dirty look when I was worried about a work problem. But even though your emotions *feel* real, that doesn't mean they're right. You may feel I'm mad at you when I'm not. You may believe I don't care when I do. You may feel worried, afraid, or rejected, but that was never my intention. These are your interpretations and perceptions, and even though they *feel* real, that doesn't mean they're right. I ask you one thing: when you feel like I don't love you or that I am angry with you or frustrated with you, please come and talk to me about what you are feeling. I might mess up at times, but I want you to know that I am *for you.*"

My kids listened intently, and I could tell my words made a difference.

As kids grow older, we can continue to teach them about emotions. As I've said over and over throughout this book, emotional awareness needs to be learned. It's important to remind our kids that no matter what their emotions are telling them, they can learn to control their behavior.

Focus on the Behavior, Not the Feelings

"Many parents make the mistake of assuming that since their child's behavior is connected to their feelings, fixing the *feelings* will fix the behavior. Unfortunately, nothing could be further from the truth," wrote James Lehman.[3] When children are overwhelmed, it's not the time to tell them that they need to fix their feelings.

Otherwise they'll believe you're saying that their emotions aren't valid. Instead of telling kids that they shouldn't *feel* as they do, label their emotions and talk with them about their behavior. Let them know there is a better way to respond. For example, instead of saying, "Don't get angry at your brother," say, "You are angry, but don't yell at your brother. You may talk to him when you are calm and caring." Also, before a moment of crisis, teach your preteen *how* to become calm and caring again. Brainstorm ideas together. You might sit down with your preteen and talk about a recent time when he was angry.

Good questions to ask in this discussion are:

- How did you feel when that happened?
- How did you respond?
- What was the outcome?
- How could you respond better next time?

Preteens might have some good ideas about how they could respond better the next time, but often we have to give them additional suggestions for how to calm themselves, such as finding a quiet place, taking deep breaths, or squeezing a stress ball. We can also encourage our preteens to create calming cards that list their own ideas of things that could help them calm down.

What Is beneath the Upset?

Probably one of the most useful skills we can teach our preteens is how to express what's going on underneath the upset. We sometimes teach young children how to use their words but then forget to build on that by teaching older kids good communication skills as well.

Preteens need to be taught to state their thoughts and desires instead of expecting others to magically read their minds. For example, when I notice one of my preteens becoming irritated, I ask whether she has something she needs to share. "You have to help us by stating what you're thinking and what you want. We can't read your mind. What's going on?" In the beginning I had to help my preteens find the words. "If you'd like your sibling to turn down the television, ask. If you want help with your homework, ask." When kids can communicate their desires, they are working to solve a problem with another person instead of just letting anger build inside.

Preteens also need to learn that listening is part of healthy communication. I often say, "I have something I want to talk to you about—or ask you—but I need you to listen. When I am done, then I will give you a chance to respond." When preteens know they will have a chance to talk, they are more willing to listen.

Of course, communication needs to go both ways. Just as it's important for preteens to learn to listen, it's important for us to listen to them. I like how Dr. Laura Markham put it on Aha! Parenting:

> If you can stay calm and listen for what's going on underneath [your child's] upset, you can use it as an opportunity to get closer. You could respond to her raising her voice at you by angrily insisting on respect, but you would drive your daughter away. Not knowing what to do with their tumultuous feelings, tweens and teens often act out towards the

people they feel safest with: their parents. If we get distracted by their disrespect, or react angrily, we miss the real message. If we can instead empathize, look for the upset under the disrespect, and remind them of who they really are ("You don't usually act unkindly"), we create an opening to help them manage their feelings.[4]

A Soft Place to Land

Even though my kids' preteen years are hard for me, I'm learning to give them what they need from me. Sometimes that means talking and listening. Other times it means snuggling as we watch a movie or offering a hug. I've found that just because my preteens are growing taller and their bodies have started to change, that doesn't mean they don't want affection. They still like hugs. They still like me to invite them to sit next to me on movie night. Affection is communication too.

And when it comes to dealing with eye rolls, bad attitudes, and "Whatever," I've learned there is something even better than simply walking away without lecturing. When I see an attitude coming or frustration and anger rising, one of the best things I can do is draw near to my preteen daughter and ask, "Would you like a hand with that task? Would you like some help?" It's amazing how quickly her anger fades when she knows I am on her side.

That's the most important thing, really.

Our preteens need to know that we are their biggest fans. It's a role we can fill better than anyone else. Preteens often try to grow up too soon; they want to be independent. Just knowing that in us they have a soft place to land can lessen their anxiety about all the changes happening in their world. And this soft place can turn out to be a strong foundation for the teen years to come.

Reflection Questions

1. What are some ways you can prepare yourself to avoid escalating with your preteen when it's obvious that he wants to pull you into his anger?

2. In what areas can you give your preteen more space and more choices to make so he can learn how to be more responsible? How can you prepare yourself to release some of the control?

3. Do your preteens know you are *for* them (lovingly seeking the very best for them)? If not, what emotions, perceptions, or interpretations may need to be discussed? In what ways will reminding your preteen that you are for him help him overcome some of his anger? Finally, how can you become a soft place for your preteen to land?

Action Steps

1. To avoid power struggles, make a short list of nonnegotiables for your preteen. Let your preteen know the requirements. Post them where they will be regularly seen. Also, make a list for yourself of

things you'll choose not to let yourself worry about, things to let go.

2. Make time to talk with your preteen. Set aside a special time together or free up your evening, around bedtime, knowing it's a time when your preteen will most likely want to talk. Open your heart to talking about whatever your child wants to tell you, whether it be little and ordinary things or something vulnerable and emotionally significant.

3. Talk to your preteen about the changes happening in his life with all the classes, teachers, and new expectations. Offer to go over your child's weekly schedule to talk about responsibilities, organization, and time management. Be your preteen's advocate instead of simply being another person with high expectations and demands.

11

CALMING TEEN ANGER

My daughter sat on the couch, knees pressed to her chest, chewing on her fingernails. If anyone other than a parent had spotted her, that person would have thought she was watching the Disney movie her younger siblings were glued to, but I knew otherwise. I'd just told her I wasn't going to drive her to her friend's house that evening. When she continued to argue, I threatened to take away her phone for the day if she kept up the bad attitude. She'd stopped arguing, but anger simmered inside. Sure enough, for the rest of that day—and the next—she went through the motions of interacting with our family, yet when another conflict came up, she was still angry. "You never let me do what I want!"

Some of my kids are screamers, while others let their anger simmer under the surface. By the time kids become teens, they've learned that showing their anger often gets them into trouble. So they hold it inside. But their anger doesn't dissipate. It stacks and multiplies until the teen either has an angry outburst or makes destructive choices—such as alcohol, drugs, self-harm, or unhealthy relationships—in an effort to ease the pain.

Of course, it's easier for us as adults to understand what happens when our kids don't deal with their anger than it is to explain it to a teen. The teen years are when children are most likely to resist our help, information, or advice. They are attempting to become independent, and they may resent parenting. They think they know better. They think parents don't understand. Yet when teens are angry, we know that deep down there's a lot going on. And when they express their anger, we parents are often the target.

Remember, your teen's anger isn't personal—it's not about you, even if she targets you as her problem. You're the adult, and your teen wants and needs you to model adult behavior. Be respectful to your child, and you'll build trust and respect in return.

Look at Yourself First

Teens know how to express their anger in sharp, harsh words. Too often their words shoot like arrows, piercing parents' hearts. And parents often shoot angry words right back. Our teens' words hurt us, and we want them to know it. We find it all too easy to point out our teens' faults. Soon there are two wounded people, aching and feeling unloved. I know. I've been there.

When you and your teen have exchanged angry words, it's important to deal with your own emotions before dealing with your teen's. Ask yourself, *Have I committed to sticking it out with my teen and walking with her through the hard stuff? Am I approaching my child from a place of truth? Am I speaking what I believe God would want me to say—and what my teen needs to hear—even though*

it may be challenging? Am I committed to watching my words no mat-
ter what lies and accusations my teen hurls at me?

One thing's for sure: verbal spars with teens never lead to any good. You'll never regret the hurtful words you *held back*, but if you let harsh words slip out, they will wound your teen all the way into adulthood.

Sadly, sometimes wounding words are a pattern families pass on for generations. If you are struggling to communicate with your teen in a healthy way, you may need to step back, sit before God, and reflect. Is it possible that you are passing on wounding words from your own parents? If so, ask God to show you whether you have hurts that need healing. Perhaps you'll discover you have more pain than you know how to work through alone. This may be a good time to seek help from a counselor or life coach. It's amazing how beneficial outside help can be, and when we take time to deal with the hurts and struggles in our own lives, we will be better able to help our teens with theirs.

Pay attention to how you react to your teen. Are you a safe place for your child? When she confides in you about something she has done or is struggling with, how do you respond? Do you get angry? Try to fix things? Take things personally? Launch into a lecture? If so, then it's only understandable that your teen is keeping her distance. Thankfully, it's never too late to rebuild your relationship. This happens when you soften your ways and act with control, love, and respect.

Currently, with four teens in the house, my goal is to treat them respectfully by speaking the truth in love. With God's strength, this is possible. I know, because I've asked Him to help me control my tongue, and He has. I asked Him to help me recall hurtful words that were spoken to me when I was a child, and when He did, I was reminded how much even offhanded comments can sting. Then I asked Him to show me my heart. I prayed Psalm 139:23–24: "Search me, O God, and know my heart; test me and know my anxious thoughts. Point out anything in me that offends you, and lead me along the path of everlasting life" (NLT).

I also considered Psalm 19:12: "How can I know all the sins lurking in my heart? Cleanse me from these hidden faults" (NLT). God answered this prayer, showing me that I'm not a perfect parent helping imperfect kids. Instead, we are five people in need of God's help. This awareness has helped me approach my teens with humility and grace.

In addition to working on our own hearts, we need to take time to talk with our teens—to figure out what's really going on in their hearts.

Talk with Teens, Not at Them

Ignored emotions are like walls between teens and parents. Of course, "talking things through" doesn't mean sitting down and demanding your teen talks to you. The best way to communicate with your teen is simply to spend time with her. Ask her to run errands with you. Take her out to lunch. Take a long drive together. The best conversations happen after all the small talk is out of the way. Then, when your teen feels comfortable and senses a connection with you, she will be more likely to open up—usually about things you had no idea were going on inside her.

If you are spending time with your teen—and she still isn't opening up—she may be attempting to gain control through silence. You may need to loosen the reins and give her slack to make more of her own decisions about her basic responsibilities, like homework, chores, and bedtime.

To help our children gain responsibility, we must offer them opportunities to be responsible rather than ordering them to do what we think is responsible.[1] When the parent controls the teenager's life to the extreme, making all decisions for her, the teenager feels powerless. The teen is unable to develop independence and self-identity and believes silence is the only way to gain the upper hand. "With silence, the teenager is in control, at least for the moment," explained Gary Chapman, author of *The 5 Love Languages of Teenagers.* "When the parent panics and woefully moans that the teenager will not talk, or when the parent verbally explodes and says loudly, 'I can't help you if you don't tell me what's wrong,' the teenager is winning the battle—because she is out of your control."[2]

Also, in the middle of a conflict, don't bring up past issues that might remain unresolved. Instead, talk about one thing at a time. Ask, "What's going on?" Then be brave enough to tenderly share how you see things. "This is how I see the situation. I'd like to hear how you see it …"

For example, when it comes to conflicts over movies, music, and other media choices, I tell my teens what I think, but I also listen. I give them a chance to explain what attracts them to a song or why they want to watch a movie. Sometimes, when I look into it, the media is more innocent than I first thought. But I also tell them when I don't think the media is good for them and why. I've said to my kids many times, "When you listen to those types of lyrics, they not only enter your brain, but they also lodge deep in your heart. I can still remember all the words to the songs that I listened to in high school—and most of them are not good messages. I don't believe that's what you want to have stick with you for the rest of your life."

It may seem as though your teen doesn't want your input or doesn't respect your opinion, but we never know what words will linger in our children's minds. I've often heard my kids repeating my words to others: "You know, I just don't think that movie is good for me" or "Even though the tune is good, the words aren't. I have better things to listen to." When we focus on each issue as it comes, with care and consideration, our teens notice and sometimes even pass on our advice to their friends.

But what if, despite all your attempts to talk with your teen about her feelings, she remains distant or even defiant? To find the answer, we'll look at two ways most teens display their anger.

Helping Teens with Implosive Anger

Most teenagers lean toward one of two approaches to anger: implosive or explosive, meaning either inward or outward focused. Implosion may appear easier to deal with. A silent teenager seems easier to handle than a loud, angry, and confrontational one. Yet with implosion a teen holds her anger inside and it remains unprocessed. As Katherina says in Shakespeare's *The Taming of the Shrew*, "My tongue will tell the anger of my heart, / Or else my heart concealing it will break."[3] Is your teen walking around with an angry, broken heart?

Teens who hold everything inside and refuse to deal with their anger—or other emotions—often do so because they fear what will come out if they speak the truth. They may be afraid to tell a parent that they are being bullied or feeling angry over a breakup or about a family member's divorce. They worry that once the truth comes out, they won't be able to control their emotions or anger. They fear that with the smallest release of emotions, a flood will break forth, and then their anger will lead to trouble or hurting those around them.

Sometimes teens may not even know the whole truth about anger. They may view their anger as wrong and therefore unsafe to express. They may believe only bad kids get angry. When this is the case, a teen will often suppress these emotions, not understanding the emotions she is attempting to lock deep inside are holding her hostage.

Teens with passive, or implosive, anger express that emotion through indirect actions. They may try to wound or manipulate others. They might hold back their opinions and feelings. They may mumble under their breath or speak quietly. They often struggle to make eye contact and may slouch. Even if they agree with you with their words, their attitude, sighs, and body language communicate just the opposite. The answer given to requests is "Yes," but the behavior is "No."

For most teens this behavior displays itself in simple ways: "Yes, I'll finish my homework before I play video games—I know what you've told me a million times …" The teen doesn't want to say no to your request, yet she has no intention of doing it. She's just pushing off conflict to a later time.

Taken to the extreme, however, suppressed anger can turn into passive-aggressive behavior. The behavior of a teen with passive-aggressive anger might look a bit different. You'll hear, "Fine. I hope you're happy. Yeah, sure I'll use the last of my money to put gas in the car since I went over on my data." But then the car doesn't get filled and the data usage isn't watched the next month, and your teen also stomps around as if you're the one who did something to hurt her.

Passive-aggressive teens undermine parents' authority again and again. Ross Campbell, author of *How to Really Love Your Angry Child*, explained it this way:

> Passive aggression's purpose as a reaction is primarily to upset the parents or other authority figures. We may try any strategy to correct the behavior, but it's not going to work. As a matter of fact, the more effort the parents put into curbing the behavior, the more determined will be the child's efforts to upset them. And because the actions are illogical and irrational, the parents almost always will be upset. This makes the passive-aggressive child feel successful, and he or she will step up efforts to cause even more frustration. The most common areas of combat in children are usually grades and values.[4]

Sadly, when passive-aggressive teens strike out at parents, teachers, and other authority figures by their behavior, *the teens end up as the big losers*. Teens' snarky attitudes may rob them of friends. Poor grades will hold them back. They may make destructive choices as a way to hurt those around them and to numb the depressed emotions and hidden anger building inside, but they also reap the fallout of that destruction.

"Some individuals move into more serious kinds of passive-aggressive behavior through drugs, alcohol, disease, poverty, or even suicide, the ultimate passive-aggressive behavior," Campbell added.[5] If your teen's choices are more destructive than lower grades and a messy room—things like substance abuse, self-harm, or eating disorders—seek professional help. Passive-aggressive behavior should not be ignored.

Not every child with implosive anger is passive aggressive. I learned this when talking to one of my girls' therapists. I sat in her office, listing complaints about my daughter's passive anger, just as I'd done with other issues. She looked at me and offered an understanding smile. "You know, a lot of the issues you've worked through have been because of your kids' trauma, because of triggers, or because of biological issues. There have been behaviors we can label as coming from 'an angry kid,' but some things—like this passive anger—are normal, teenage stuff."

She explained that in early adolescence, ages thirteen to fifteen, children tend to hold everything in, including anger, and they may act out in passive, angry ways. They may agree to a request but then delay acting on it. This is the child who agrees to take out the trash but still hasn't done it two hours later. She may forget to do homework she never wanted to do in the first place. But as long as the behavior hurts no one and causes no damage, we may consider it "normal" for this stage. It is not a sign of simmering rage.

I'm currently raising my seventh child who has gone through this age, and I can attest to the dawdling, doing a poor job on chores, the messy room, and the carelessness. Even though it's hard, the best way to deal with passive anger is to sit down with your child when things are going well, tell her what you see, and offer consequences for continued inaction. Make it clear what needs to be done and how. Then give a time limit. For example, if your child has refused to clean her room for weeks on end, let her know she has until Friday to clean it or she loses her phone or computer until it's done. A reasonable time frame and reasonable consequences won't guarantee your child will comply, but she will learn accountability.

Also, offer a reward for a job well done. We are rewarded in all areas of life—with paychecks, special acknowledgments, and accolades. We shouldn't withhold the same from our children. I'll often reward my teens with a pizza night or a little something they've been wanting, like nail polish or an iTunes gift card, for a job well done.

Helping Teens with Explosive Anger

While kids with implosive anger hold their anger in, explosive teens let it out. Parents of these teens have no problem getting their kids to communicate. The challenge comes when teens do so in the wrong way—when they yell, scream, throw things, hit, and threaten.

"Anger is what we call a cover-up emotion, a sign that says something is wrong. But the real problem is always underneath," said Dr. Lynn Weiss, psychotherapist and author of several book son ADHD. "Anger is like a shield that a [child] uses to protect himself, to cover vulnerable feelings—feelings of loss, shame, helplessness, hopelessness, or fear."[6] It's easier to be angry and keep everyone at arm's length. As parents we may know this, but it still can be hard to deal with explosive anger.

To keep a teen's anger from affecting you takes a lot of patience. But remember, your kid's anger is rarely about you. And as much as teens tell you they don't want your help, your help *is* what your teen needs—your calm, loving, and attentive help.

"The teen learns to process anger by experience," wrote Gary Chapman. "We start where the teenager is now and help our son or daughter process anger even if it involves listening to the teen's initial screams. Later we can teach better methods of communicating anger. But we must never allow the teen's language to keep us from listening to the teen's message."[7] When we as parents are angry or frustrated, we are not listening. Instead, we are thinking about what to say and how to respond. We interrogate, threaten, lecture, and reprimand. This never helps.

We especially won't get through to externally angry teens when their emotions are piqued. "The wise parent will focus on what the teen is saying, not the manner in which she is saying it," said Chapman. "If the teen is yelling at you, she is trying to tell you something. The wise parent will shift into the listening mode. I suggest that you reach for paper and pen and begin to record what you hear the teenager saying."[8]

When I read these words, I feel a bit convicted. I need this reminder. If I lose my cool with my teens, I am not listening to them. If I tell them to shut their mouths, I'm not listening. If I refute everything my teens say, I'm not listening. If I'm justifying myself and my responses, I'm not listening. Ouch! Here's the thing:

when we listen without reacting, we can hear what's really going on with our child. We can ask ourselves, "What is the truth behind my child's words?"

If a teen's words get out of hand or turn disrespectful or threatening, it's appropriate to take a break from the conversation or to give consequences. (One of my favorite parenting websites is LoveandLogic.com, which provides a bounty of resources that explain how to handle children and teens in a way that is both loving and logical. Check it out for more in-depth help in providing appropriate consequences.) When we assign consequences after the anger in the situation has passed, teens are more likely to accept them and—believe it or not—perceive them as a form of protection. They know we won't let them go too far with their anger and they will have to deal with the consequences if they do.

When dealing with angry, aggressive teens, the best tactics are those we've already discussed.

1. Be there for your teen and remember her anger most likely isn't about you.

2. Let your teen know the rules and your expectations.

3. Establish boundaries and set consequences for angry outbursts. An appropriate consequence might be losing media privileges or not being able to go to the movies with friends.

4. Work with your teen to discover triggers and keep an anger log. What makes her angry at age fifteen will most likely be different than what made her angry at age eleven.

5. Help your teen identify healthy ways to release her anger. Maybe it's going for a run, taking a shower, or squeezing a stress ball. Maybe it's just putting in earbuds or retreating to her room to have quiet and space to calm down.

These are all useful for addressing explosive behavior, but watch for warning signs that teens have serious anger issues. If they are talking about weapons, playing violent video games, issuing threats, or acting out aggressively, then seek professional help. Also monitor for other at-risk behaviors such as drugs, sex, drinking, self-harming, and other dangerous or illegal behavior. These are all signs of deeper underlying problems, whether anger is displayed inwardly or outwardly.

Keep in mind that while the teen years can be demanding, adolescence is simply a season in your child's life. Just because things are difficult now does not mean they always will be from here on out. Even if you don't do everything right, you can approach parenting challenges with words of humility and words of life.

Words of Humility and Words of Life

If we want a foundation to build on as our teens grow into adults, it is important to speak words of humility and words of life to our kids.

Modeling is a huge part of effective parenting. Teens, more than any other age, know when you are not "walking your talk" and when you have blown it. Instead of acting as if you have your act together, confess your failures to your teens and share the changes you want to make in your life. Here are some of the things we need to be willing to say to our kids:

- "I have not listened, but I want to be a better listener."
- "I have overreacted, but I want to remain calm and be a steady support to you."
- "I tend to take things personally, but I want to give you the benefit of the doubt."
- "I have often brushed aside your feelings, but I want you to know that your feelings are valid, even angry feelings."
- "I have argued with you about the facts without paying attention to your feelings. I want to be more concerned about your heart."

Can you imagine your teen's outer defenses crumbling as she hears you admitting your mistakes and expressing how you want to change?

Also remember the power of life-giving words. It's so easy to speak "curses" over our children. Not curse words, but things like "You are so out of control" or "You don't have your head on straight." Proverbs 18:21 says, "The tongue can bring death or life; those who love to talk will reap the consequences" (NLT). The New International Version says, "The tongue has the power of life and death, and those who love it will eat its fruit."

"We all eat the fruit of our words," said my friend Francie. "Whatever we speak, we reap. Words are part of the image-bearing nature we have as people of God. In Genesis, God spoke and a world was created. When Jesus came, He spoke and people were healed and hearts were changed. We carry that same power by our words."

When we say, "Why are you so out of control? Why don't you just get a grip?" our children believe what they hear: they *are* out of control and can't get a grip. As parents we can ask God to rewrite our vocabulary to give us words of life to speak. Know who your teens are and speak encouragement over them: "You have a powerful heart, a compassionate nature, and God has given you self-control." If we speak things like this enough times, our teens will start to believe them.

It's these words that our teens will carry into adulthood. And hopefully it's these words that will help them leave their unhealthy anger behind as they become adults.

Reflection Questions

1. How do you respond to your teen? Are you a safe place, or do you tend to react in ways that push your teen away?
2. Does your teen deal more with inwardly directed (implosive) or outwardly directed (explosive) anger? What warning signs do you see, if any?
3. What words of life can you speak to your teen?

Action Steps

1. Make a plan to spend time with your teen. Think of fun, nonthreatening things you can do together.

2. Sit down with your teen and be honest and humble about how you have responded to your child and how you've handled your own anger. Commit to your teen to do things differently.

3. Make a list of ways you can help your teen deal with her anger, whether implosive or explosive. If your child is acting out in destructive ways, find a professional who can help.

12

A HEALING PLACE FOR ADOPTED AND FOSTER KIDS

I was taken aback when the trauma therapist barely gave my angry son a sideways glance and instead focused on me as we sat in her office. "What do you think about your son? How would you describe him in three words?"

I paused. Was this a test? A dozen words flashed through my mind, none of them positive. I took a deep breath, and I gave three descriptors that were accurate yet didn't make me look like a bad mom: "Active, willful, and destructive."

At nearly three years old, Buddy was all those things and more. He never stopped moving. He always fought for his own way and seemed bent on breaking everything he could get his hands on. If I tried to calm him or corral him or teach him to be gentle, he'd get mad. It was hard to find peace with such a willful child.

"And how do you *feel* about him?" the therapist continued.

Again I tried to think of ways to share what was happening without sounding like a horrible mom for not adoring my son. "Uh,

I think he's a cute kid. I'm thankful he's in my family, but when he's around, it's just a lot of work. I mean, I love him …" My words trailed off.

The therapist didn't stop there. "And tell me about what you thought when you first saw a picture of him?"

I thought back to that moment. I was in Colorado Springs that day, recording a broadcast for Focus on the Family when my husband texted me with the news and then emailed a photo of the children the adoption specialist was asking us to consider.

"He looked … awkward. He had a bad haircut, and I could tell by the photo someone was trying to hold him so he'd stand still. Even from the photo he looked like he'd be a lot of work."

The therapist listened, and I expected some type of lecture. Instead, she told me she had a plan for Buddy's therapy—something we'd do together. For the next six months, I was to focus on the one-on-one ritual with Buddy I described in chapter 6, where I noticed him, repeated his words, and praised him.

At first the task made no sense. What did *this* have to do with my son's behavior? But then, after four months of spending one-on-one time with my son, I realized that each joyful moment spent together brought us closer. Looking back, I see now the activity the therapist had us do was not just for Buddy but also for me. Only with time, focus, praise, attention, and fun could our relationship grow. Buddy is now seven years old. He's still active and willful at times, but he's also smart and thoughtful and caring. I'd do anything for that kid now, and his hugs are one of my favorite things. But it's been a journey—a journey toward deep love that I'm thankful I dared to embark on.

Our kids moved into our home with varying levels of issues, and they all struggled with anger. I wish I could say I loved all seven of them immediately and equally, but that isn't the case. Love isn't something you can turn off and on. Love needs time to be planted, take root, and grow. While my love for each of them is now strong, it grew over time.

We adoptive parents have such high hopes when we adopt a child and bring that child home. Some of us thought about fostering and adopting for years, and even when we took the training classes, we imagined *our* love will make all the difference. In many ways it does, yet even more vital is a parent's commitment to help a child heal from the pain of his past, pain that often exhibits itself as anger.

In his book *Taking Charge of ADHD*, Russell A. Barkley shared some advice given by a wonderful and wise retired teacher that has stuck with me: "The children who need love the most will always ask for it in the most unloving ways."[1] I've found this to be true.

Throughout this book, I've shared several ways my kids have exhibited anger, but there are many stories I haven't shared. I can honestly say that anger—in various forms—for many years was a daily, unwelcome guest in our home. We dealt with it in big and small ways. Anger affected every part of our lives.

John and I opened our home to foster care and adoption with a lot of hope and little knowledge of what the reality would look like. The good news is we had to deal with the anger only one moment at a time, hour by hour and day by day. It's not that we enjoyed any part of dealing with the anger, but learning to help our kids find calm was an important part of bringing our family together. Anger indicated what was happening inside my kids, inside their hearts. It unmasked other emotions that could no longer remain hidden. It revealed all the places our kids needed to heal and also motivated me to help them find that healing.

Would I have been so diligent about discovering the right help for my kids if I hadn't been dealing with their daily, ugly outbursts? I don't think so.

Their anger also gave me a hint of all my children had faced in the past. The intensity of their emotion indicated the intensity of their trauma—not only before they entered state care but also while they were there. As small children, they were removed from the only home they knew and placed into the care of strangers (many different strangers), some of whom provided their best care and others of whom didn't.

As a mom trying to help these kids heal, I learned a lot about children, trauma, myself, our mutual needs, and healing. Out of everything I've learned, the following dos and don'ts top the list for how to make your home a place of healing.

1. *Don't take your adopted child's anger personally.* This point bears repeating, because it is very difficult to do all you can to love and help your child, only to be rejected and confronted by anger day after day.

When one of our kids blew up over a big or small thing, I would get hurt and offended and wonder what I'd done wrong. I'd think through my actions to try to figure out what would make my child reject me or lash out. I wanted to shout, "I've done so much work to make this adoption happen. I've given so much! I've poured myself out … and this is how you treat me?" I'd also get mad because of how they made me look—incompetent. As parents we often feel guilty about and ashamed of our kids' anger. We react to their behavior as if it is our fault, and we worry that other people will believe it is.

My kids' anger showed up in many ways—shouting matches, temper tantrums, and defiance. And as I dealt with episode after episode, I discovered that all the things making my kids over-the-top angry were somehow connected to their broken pasts. As my children opened up about what they were really mad about—or about old thoughts or feelings that current issues were stirring up—I realized they weren't mad at me. Their anger had been smoldering for a long time, and my request, reaction, or reprimand was merely a gust of air that fanned the flame. My friend Megan, a mom of nine children, including two adopted kids, put it this way: "Feelings are an *indicator* not a map. If you use them as a map to direct you, then you won't like where they take you."

A friend who works at a children's psychiatric treatment facility shared the following about how adults can get children to talk about what they are feeling:

- Ask open-ended questions (questions that can't be answered with a yes or a no).
- Repeat what the child has said to validate that you heard correctly.
- Offer support either with your presence or by problem-solving with the child's input.
- Engage your child in identifying positive coping skills to manage anger. (Our family used calming cards.)

As I got to know my kids better, as I discovered their hearts and their unmet needs, I stopped worrying that their anger was all about me. Instead, I investigated how to help my children with the help of professionals and God. I used their anger to discover the places where deep healing was needed.

2. *Work on yourself as a way to help your kids.* For so long I thought caring for my heart, mind, soul, and spirit was selfish. Instead, attending to myself prepared me to offer my best to my kids. "As children develop, their brains 'mirror' their parent's brain," wrote Daniel J. Siegel and Tina Payne Bryson. "In other words, the parent's own growth and development, or lack of those, impact the child's brain. As parents become more aware and emotionally healthy, their children reap the rewards and move toward health as well."[2]

The better I was able to care for myself—making it easier for me to control my own anger and find help for my overwhelmed emotions—the better I was able to assist my kids. And they were able to see in me that it is possible to calmly deal with difficult and painful feelings.

3. *Teach kids they have a right to be angry.* Adopted kids have a right to be angry—angry at the situation, angry at how they were hurt, and angry at the daily little stuff that always comes up.

"It's okay to be angry. It's okay to express it," my sister Lesley—a former foster mom—reminded me. "I would tell my foster kids to go to their room and scream into their pillow if they felt out-of-control angry, to get out the brunt of their emotions, and then we could talk it through. Sometimes they just needed to scream a little."[3]

"Emotions aren't good or bad. They just *are*," commented my friend Tara on one of my Facebook posts. "It's okay to be angry. It's not okay to stuff it down and let it fester into bitterness, resentment, and poor decisions that lead to life-altering choices."

"Each person's feelings are real. Rejecting, invalidating, or minimizing a person's feelings is rejecting that person's reality," wrote attorney and peacemaking expert Douglas Noll.[4] His words make sense. Every time I tried to handle my children's actions without dealing with their feelings, it confirmed in their minds that their feelings didn't matter. To them, it seemed I was like everyone else who tried to control them but didn't really care. It was only as I gave my children permission to get angry about the things that had happened to them—and got angry along with them—that they began to trust me. When they saw me getting mad about the hard things they faced, such as the neglect, abuse, and lack of care by other adults, they believed I really cared.

4. *Be teachable.* I remember sitting at our first adoption training, thinking, *I don't know why I'm here. I write parenting books. This is a waste of time!* I laugh now to think how prideful I was. Yet the first time I went to trauma therapy with our daughter Sissy, the therapist was an intern who couldn't have been more than twenty-five years old. When she started to explain why things worked and didn't work with Sissy, I was amazed. I pulled out a notebook and pen and started taking notes. It truly was a humbling experience—me (an experienced mom) taking advice from a young intern. But as we adopted more kids, I learned something important: to be teachable.

"One of the very first, most basic steps to breaking any destructive pattern or to even improve in general is to have a teachable heart," my friend Trisha reminded me when I was going through a hard time. "What is the condition of my heart? Am I willing to learn? Am I willing to admit my wrongs? Am I willing to admit I need help? Am I willing to accept help? Am I willing to hear correction without getting defensive? Am I willing to try new things? Am I willing to use someone else's ideas and suggestions?" I knew she was right, but her questions challenged me.

As I became willing to read books about helping adopted kids and as I sought therapists' advice, the atmosphere in our home began to change. When I was open to receiving help and advice, I learned how to help my kids.

5. *Understand that shame is at the heart of anger issues.* I've never felt more incapable and powerless than I did when dealing with an angry, out-of-control child. That feeling brought a flood of panic. *I can't do this. I can't control this situation. I don't have what it takes.*

All adoptive parents reach a moment when we think, *I am not enough.* When all our fears and worries about being a bad parent come crashing down around us. *I'm a fraud. Why did I ever think I could do this? I'm going to ruin this kid for life.* And then, out of this sense of shame, we project all our feelings of unworthiness onto our kids. "As I often tell patients, 'Shamed people shame people,'" wrote Curt Thompson, author of *The Soul of Shame.* "Long before we are criticizing others, the source of that criticism has been planted, fertilized and grown in our own lives, directed at ourselves, and often in ways we are mostly unaware of."[5]

Once I realized that shame was at the core of my feelings of not being enough, I knew I had to change. I started focusing on what I did right, instead of all the things I thought I was doing wrong. The less I criticized myself, the less I criticized my kids. And whenever I noticed my kids feeling as if they weren't enough, I reminded them of who God created them to be. I reminded them to speak words of truth and encouragement to themselves, instead of letting critical thoughts play over and over in their minds. Only truth overcomes shame—in my heart and in my kids' hearts.

6. *Show up every day.* It's important to look past your child's behavior to find his heart. Even if there is only a crack in the armor your child has erected, fill that place with love.

Showing up means not giving up. Children who are in foster care and who've been adopted have experienced great loss and have faced trauma. Trauma changes the brain's structure and makeup, and children often get stuck developmentally at the age the trauma happened. The later the trauma happens, the less resilient the child is and the harder it is for that child to make positive changes in his life.

The best way to help our adopted kids is to be there for them in good times and in bad. Sticking with my kids—even in the midst of the hard stuff—brought a lot of healing on its own.

7. *Give up preconceived notions about medication and treatment.* The first time I met with my children's doctor, I wanted to know when I could take my kids off the medications they were on for hyperactivity, ADHD, anxiety, and depression. I believed that a stable home and loving parents should make them all better. While over time we were able to take our kids off some of their medications, it wasn't as simple as I expected. It required working with doctors and testing how my kids did at lower doses. It also meant understanding that some of our kids will likely need to take medications for the rest of their lives. I learned to be open minded about my kids' needs. I learned to listen to experts who helped me understand.

Adopted kids are often given medications to address physical and chemical issues, such as anxiety and depression. Child abuse can cause psychological ramifications for many years. According to MentalHelp.net, "Victimized people commonly develop emotional or psychological problems secondary to their abuse, including anxiety disorders and various forms of depression. They may develop substance abuse disorders. If abuse has been very severe, the victim may be traumatized, and may develop a posttraumatic stress injury such as posttraumatic stress disorder (PTSD), or acute stress disorder."[6] Abuse alone is not sufficient to create psychological disorders, but it can be a strong factor contributing to them. Know that doctors are there to provide help. The fact that your child may need medications indicates what your child has faced and does not indicate that you lack the ability to help him.

Research the medical options and be open to a doctor's help and advice. Most of my adopted kids are still taking various medications, but I believe they are for our children's own good. Trust that, if needed, the right medications can help your child, allowing him to find stability and bringing more peace to your home.

8. *Meet your kids where they are.* When our five-year-old daughter Sissy moved in with us, I knew I had to connect with her despite her behavioral issues. I made a point of sitting down with her and playing every day. I'd bring out all types of interesting toys, but the thing she wanted to do most was to play baby. Not with baby dolls. She wanted to *be the baby*. That was the only thing she wanted to play. She wanted me to dress and undress her. She wanted me to hold her, rock her, sing songs, and play peek a boo. She wanted me

to pretend to put diapers on her. We played this multiple times a day, and she got angry when I didn't want to play.

I remember talking about this with her therapist. "What are you doing when she wants to play baby?" the therapist asked.

"I play along."

"Wonderful. That's exactly what she needs. Even though she's not conscious of it, she missed out on something. Once she receives what is missed, she'll move on."

The therapist was right. Something inside my daughter needed to be fixed—something I could help with by providing her with the care and attention that she had missed as an infant. Sissy and I played baby for months, and then my daughter moved on and began asking me to play different games with her. I started where she was and helped my daughter move forward.

"For many years, I had a refrigerator magnet that was a cracked eggshell graphic and the words, 'It's much easier to build strong children than repair cracked adults,'" wrote Yyuvone Heidelberger, reginal coordinator for The CALL. She went on to say, "In a perfect world this might be true, but in my world, the children who came to my home were already broken. They came in my front door with a trash bag and an imaginary suitcase full of their broken dreams and dashed hopes. I once told a foster daughter that even though I didn't know her, I did know that out of her broken shell will emerge a soft, baby chick who will need a [mama] chicken to teach her how to be a baby chick. I wasn't going to try to glue her back together. I was going to take her as she is and help her start from that point and move forward."[7]

If, for any reason, adoptive children have missed a developmental stage, they might need a way to fill in that area. When you take time to meet your child right where he is, a bond is formed. These bonds connect parents and children, helping kids overcome anger issues.

This is true for older children too. My daughter, who moved in with us at eleven years old, wanted me to help her dry off and blow-dry her hair after her showers. During this time, she was thrilled when I played peek a boo with her. She giggled like a toddler. She loved toddler songs, finger games, and being tickled. By her behavior, I knew she'd missed a lot of attention and nurture as a baby and toddler. This made sense, since she was born as the fifth baby to a twenty-two-year-old mom. By meeting my daughter's needs, I allowed her to bond with me.

9. *Try essential oils.* I ignored my sister-in-law Sandy the first dozen times she mentioned trying essential oils to help my kids with their anger problems. Then, after I'd faced a particularly hard and frustrating day, Sandy told me she was going to drive to our house the next day to try essential oils on my kids. Sandy lives six hours away, yet she insisted on coming. My kids were excited about seeing their cousins, and they were eager to see what Aunt Sandy was bringing them. I didn't get my hopes up. I just didn't understand how essential oils could help with anger issues.

After Sandy arrived, she told our girls to line up, and she set out some oils to rub on the bottoms of their feet. Before she'd arrived, we'd had a hard day. There'd been a lot of bickering between kids and some big blowups. I questioned how this would turn out.

The girls giggled as Sandy rubbed essential oils on their feet. They loved the physical touch. (Who wouldn't want a foot massage?)

They also delighted in all the aromas. "Oh, that smells so good." They enjoyed sniffing the bottles and deciding which they loved best.

The oils had names like Peace and Calming and Joy. Sandy told me that God placed good things in nature to benefit us and that essential oils are distilled from plants. For example, orange oil is cold-pressed from oranges, and when diffused into the air, it helps people become more alert and better able to concentrate. Lavender oil is known to have a calming effect. Eucalyptus, clove, and thyme oils are used to fight bacteria. Was it possible that there were oils that could really help my kids' anxiety and anger?

The evidence says that they could. Not long after the foot massages, I noticed my kids' attitudes changed. The grumpiness disappeared and smiles lit their faces. One of my teen daughters got especially giddy. She jumped up and began to spin around the room. "I feel like a cat on catnip!" I watched in amazement, waiting for them to tell me they were just playing. Essential oils have continued to bring feelings of peace and joy to my kids day after day.

10. *Share your broken story.* When our older adopted kids first started visiting our home over weekends, we learned a lot about them—their likes and dislikes, their hopes and fears. How? Something triggered a memory, and they launched into a story. We learned about how they ended up in foster care, their first days of school, the challenges they faced, and the events that molded their personalities.

In addition to telling their stories, our girls often asked us to tell ours. It never failed that after they got ready for bed, they'd want to hear a story about us, about our lives. By sharing our stories with our kids, we helped them understand our family culture.

Have you shared important stories from your life with your kids? If not, here a few ideas to start with:

- The story of your salvation. Your children may think you always believed in God, never struggled, or never questioned your need for God in your life. If they don't know your faith story, when they have doubts, struggles, and questions, they may think they are all alone. Share how you came to believe in Jesus and how you chose to dedicate your life to Him. If you became a Christian at a young age, share about other faith steps you took as you grew older. How did your faith change and grow throughout the years?

- A story of a vivid childhood memory. It's hard for our children to picture us as kids, yet our childhood shaped who we are. One vivid memory I've shared is the time my stepdad dropped me off at the wrong house for a birthday party when I was five years old. I didn't know the family and had no way to contact my parents. I ended up walking a few miles to my aunt's house while someone from the house I'd been dropped off at drove behind me the whole way. That story gives a hint about my childhood, and it also explains a bit of my independent streak. It also reveals why I'm so cautious with my own children. It's amazing how much one vivid, impactful event can explain.

- A story of your romance and marriage. This is one of my children's favorite stories, and they love hearing it from both me and my husband. They love asking about when we first noticed each other, our first date, and how the romance progressed. They've asked to hear the story of my husband's proposal a dozen times. Not only do we tell them about the moments that brought us together, but we also tell them about the moments that almost pushed us apart. Our stories help them understand how our relationship began and provide insights into our marriage and family today—a family they're now a part of.

- A story of your biggest regret. This is possibly the hardest story to share with my children, but it's also important. My biggest regret is having an abortion when I was fifteen years old. It's a choice I would change if I could go back in time, but it's also a choice that has affected my life and molded my decisions since. Because of this bad decision, I've dedicated a lot of time to helping others make good choices. I helped start a crisis pregnancy center, and I mentor teenage mothers. Even though it's hard sharing our regrets, it's important for our children to understand how fears and self-focus led us to make bad choices. It also humbles us and opens the doors for our kids to approach us in the future when they struggle.

- A story of when you discovered purpose. When did you discover your unique gifts and talents? How did you find your career path? What hobbies give you joy? Our adopted kids often struggle with their identity and purpose. They want to be like everyone else, even though we understand it's their uniqueness that will set them apart. Sharing stories of how you discovered your purpose will help your children understand who God created them to be.

Have I convinced you to open up with your kids about your heart and life? If so, here are just a few more short tips to help you:

- Make your stories age appropriate. You can add more to your stories over time.
- Share the good, the bad, and the ugly. Our kids already know we're not perfect. Being vulnerable encourages them to be vulnerable too.
- Don't force your story on them. If they don't seem interested, wait for a different time. My kids are often eager to hear my stories at bedtime when the house is quiet and there are no distracting electronics.
- Include God's point of view. Did your choices make God angry? Share that, but also share about His forgiveness. Can you imagine God jumping for joy at your decision? Share that too. Every

decision in our lives affects God in some way. Our children need to understand this.

The more I'm willing to open my heart and life to my children, the more willing they are to open theirs to me. We often want our kids to allow us into their lives, but this truly is a case of "Let me go first."

And that is what all this healing is about. It's opening up our hearts to our kids with a "me first" attitude. It's dealing with our kids' anger by dealing with ours. It's understanding that just as God has transformed us, He will do the same with our kids. And it's realizing that dealing with the hard stuff of anger leads us to all the good places God's wanted us to go to all along. It's a journey of healing and of hope. It's a hard journey but one I'm thankful I embarked on.

Reflection Questions

1. What does your child's anger indicate happened to him in the past? How is the intensity of his emotion an indicator of the intensity of his trauma? How does this change your opinions about his anger?

2. In what ways have your child's anger issues made you feel incompetent as a parent? In what ways have you wanted to help your child but don't know how? Where can you find encouragement to fill your heart with hope instead of doubt about your parenting?

3. In what ways can you meet your child's needs where he is today? Are there developmental milestones that

he missed? How can you meet some of those earlier needs (such as cuddling, playtime, silly songs, and finger plays) for your child?

Action Steps

1. Before we help our kids, we need to help ourselves. Make a list of resources or self-care that can help you. Choose one thing on this list to provide for yourself this week.

2. Let your child know it's okay to get mad. Together create a list of things you are mad about. This could be their past neglect or abuse or other wrongs that were done to you or those you care about. Let your child know you hurt with him. Also tell him about some of your past hurts. Together pray and ask God to bring healing to you in these areas.

3. Make a list of things you're doing right. Make a list of things your kids are doing right … and show it to them. Take time to celebrate the growth in your relationship. Perhaps make time to do this monthly so you can observe positive changes, big and small.

Conclusion

THE VICTOR'S CROWN

My teen daughter raised her voice in anger as she played a video game with her sister. The two of them were fighting over a character, and her emotions were getting heated. I could see from her face that she was about to have a meltdown.

When her dad tried to encourage her to calm down, she raised her voice at him too. Since I was sitting next to her, I leaned forward and spoke in a low tone. "Think about what you're saying and your tone. Do you need time to calm yourself?"

She sucked in a deep breath, and I watched her face relax. Then she released the breath she'd been holding. "No, I'm all right," she told me. Then, without prompting, she turned back to her sister and talked in a calm voice. John and I looked at each other. He cocked an eyebrow. I knew what he was thinking. *Is this really our kid?* It was hard to believe such a simple interaction was so effective, but the result demonstrated to us how far our daughter had come—how far we'd come. Our kids still get angry at times, but I'm amazed by how often they're able to calm themselves. Anger is an occasional visitor in our home now not a permanent resident, and I couldn't be happier.

As strange as it sounds, I am thankful for the challenge of having angry kids. Yes, my kids are different now, but so am I. I've come face-to-face with my weakness and had to depend on God more than I ever had before. This experience has trained me, and I've learned how to persevere.

My grandmother, who lives with us, has witnessed all this—the hard days and the good ones. And she is a sweet reminder that even the most difficult trials we face last only for a season. After living eighty-eight years, not only does she see the challenges our family has faced as minor, but she also knows the rewards that come with days, weeks, and years of perseverance. More than once, when I was weary and at the end of my rope, Grandma has looked at me with a twinkle in her eyes and said, "You'll get your crown someday, sweetheart. You'll get your crown."

For many years I didn't understand what she meant. I wasn't doing what I did for a crown. I didn't need a reward. Yet, as I went to God's Word, I realized what she was saying: "Blessed is the one who perseveres under trial because, having stood the test, that person will receive the crown of life that the Lord has promised to those who love him" (James 1:12).

What is the crown of life? The only other place in the Bible this phrase appears is in Revelation 2:10: "Don't be afraid of what you are about to suffer. The devil will throw some of you into prison to test you.… But if you remain faithful even when facing death, I will give you the crown of life" (NLT). Or as the New International Version translates it, "I will give you life as your victor's crown." I love Bible commentator J. Scott Duvall's explanation of what this means: "The 'victor's crown' (*stephanos*) refers to a laurel wreath presented to the athlete who endured to win the contest, rather than to a ruler's crown (*diadēma*). The victor's crown symbolizes resurrection life given by Jesus to the believer.... Throughout the Bible, God's people have always been challenged to follow him faithfully, even if it results in suffering or death. We are not supposed to seek persecution for its own sake, but neither are we to compromise in order to avoid it.... Throughout Revelation, God calls his people to faithful endurance."[1]

This is the crown I think my grandma was referring to. God calls us to finish strong, despite life's challenges, and promises to give us a victor's crown if we do. As I've faithfully endured, I have discovered a new hope for our family here on earth. We've faced many challenges, but as we've worked through them, we have grown strong together. Galatians 6:9 tells us, "Let us not become weary in doing good, for at the proper time we will reap a harvest if we do not give up." It's not just John and I who are reaping a harvest. Our children are too. As they've let down the walls around their hearts, not only have they invited John and me in more and more, but they've invited God in more too. As my children choose to follow God, they can look forward to their eternal reward, their own victor's crown.

Our greatest hope on this earth is not removal from trouble but the resurrected life to come. Knowing where our hope lies encourages me to be faithful and brings me great comfort. Knowing where my hope lies also makes me depend more on the Lord, who gives me strength. As 2 Corinthians 12:9–10 says, "Each time he said, 'My grace is all you need. My power works best in weakness.' So now I am glad to boast about my weaknesses, so that the power of Christ can work through me. That's why I take pleasure in my weaknesses, and in the insults, hardships, persecutions, and troubles that I suffer for Christ. For when I am weak, then I am strong" (NLT).

And that is what my family and I have discovered. In dealing with this weakness called anger, we've become strong.

SCRIPTURES TO MEMORIZE AS A FAMILY

One of the best things my family and I have done is memorize Scripture. When we plant God's Word in our hearts, God's truth will be available to us whenever we need it.

Self-Control and Being Slow to Anger

- "'In your anger do not sin': Do not let the sun go down while you are still angry, and do not give the devil a foothold" (Eph. 4:26–27).
- "Better a patient person than a warrior, one with self-control than one who takes a city" (Prov. 16:32).
- "Sensible people control their temper; they earn respect by overlooking wrongs" (Prov. 19:11 NLT).
- "Know this, my beloved brothers: let every person be quick to hear, slow to speak, slow to anger; for

the anger of man does not produce the righteousness of God" (James 1:19–20 ESV).

- "People with understanding control their anger; a hot temper shows great foolishness" (Prov. 14:29 NLT).
- "A hot-tempered person starts fights; a cool-tempered person stops them" (Prov. 15:18 NLT).
- "A gentle answer deflects anger, but harsh words make tempers flare" (Prov. 15:1 NLT).
- "Don't sin by letting anger control you. Think about it overnight and remain silent" (Ps. 4:4 NLT).

Forgiveness and Mercy toward Others

- "Whenever you stand praying, forgive, if you have anything against anyone, so that your Father who is in heaven will also forgive you your transgressions" (Mark 11:25 NASB).
- "Let all bitterness and wrath and anger and clamor and slander be put away from you, along with all malice. Be kind to one another, tender-hearted, forgiving each other, just as God in Christ also has forgiven you" (Eph. 4:31–32 NASB).
- "The merciful man does himself good" (Prov. 11:17 NASB).

Patience and Kindness

- "Love is patient, love is kind. It does not envy, it does not boast, it is not proud" (1 Cor. 13:4).
- "Above all, love each other deeply, because love covers over a multitude of sins" (1 Pet. 4:8).

Controlling the Tongue

- "Too much talk leads to sin. Be sensible and keep your mouth shut" (Prov. 10:19 NLT).
- "Set a guard, O LORD, over my mouth; keep watch over the door of my lips!" (Ps. 141:3 ESV).
- "Keep your tongue from evil and your lips from telling lies" (Ps. 34:13).

Depending on God's Strength

- "Each time he said, 'My grace is all you need. My power works best in weakness.' So now I am glad to boast about my weaknesses, so that the power of Christ can work through me" (2 Cor. 12:9 NLT).
- "I pray that from his glorious, unlimited resources he will empower you with inner strength through his Spirit. Then Christ will make his home in your hearts as you trust in him. Your roots will grow down into God's love and keep you strong. And

may you have the power to understand, as all God's people should, how wide, how long, how high, and how deep his love is" (Eph. 3:16–18 NLT).

- "So humble yourselves before God. Resist the devil, and he will flee from you" (James 4:7 NLT).

- "For God has not given us a spirit of fear and timidity, but of power, love, and self-discipline" (2 Tim. 1:7 NLT).

- "Stand firm against him, and be strong in your faith. Remember that your family of believers all over the world is going through the same kind of suffering you are" (1 Pet. 5:9 NLT).

God in Us

- "But the Holy Spirit produces this kind of fruit in our lives: love, joy, peace, patience, kindness, goodness, faithfulness, gentleness, and self-control. There is no law against these things" (Gal. 5:22–23 NLT).

- "Love is patient and kind. Love is not jealous or boastful or proud or rude. It does not demand its own way. It is not irritable, and it keeps no record of being wronged. It does not rejoice about injustice but rejoices whenever the truth wins out. Love never gives up, never loses faith, is always hopeful, and endures through every circumstance" (1 Cor. 13:4–7 NLT).

Appendix B

RECOMMENDED RESOURCES

Books for Parents

ADHD/Special Needs

Barkley, Russell A. *Taking Charge of ADHD: The Complete, Authoritative Guide for Parents.* New York: Guilford, 2013.

Clarkson, Sally, and Nathan Clarkson. *Different: The Story of an Outside-the-Box Kid and the Mom Who Loved Him.* Carol Stream, IL: Tyndale House, 2017.

Hallowell, Edward M., and John J. Ratey. *Driven to Distraction: Recognizing and Coping with Attention Deficit Disorder from Childhood through Adulthood.* New York: Anchor Books, 2011.

Kranowitz, Carol and Stock. *The Out-of-Sync Child: Recognizing and Coping with Sensory Processing Disorder.* New York: TarcherPerigee, 2005.

Miller, Lucy Jane. *Sensational Kids: Hope and Help for Children with Sensory Processing Disorder.* New York: Penguin Group, 2014.

Thomas, Nancy L. *When Love Is Not Enough: A Guide to Parenting Children with RAD—Reactive Attachment Disorder.* Glenwood Springs, CO: Families by Design, 2005.

Adoption

Eldridge, Sherrie. *20 Life-Transforming Choices Adoptees Need to Make.* London: Jessica Kingsley, 2015.

———. *Twenty Things Adopted Kids Wish Their Adoptive Parents Knew.* New York: Dell, 1999.

Purvis, Karyn B., David R. Cross, and Wendy Lyons Sunshine. *The Connected Child: Bring Hope and Healing to Your Adoptive Family.* New York: McGraw-Hill, 2007.

Anger

Campbell, D. Ross. *How to Really Love Your Angry Child.* With Rob Suggs. Colorado Springs: Life Journey, 2003.

Lia, Amber, and Wendy Speake. *Triggers: Exchanging Parents' Angry Reactions for Gentle Biblical Responses.* Escondido, CA: Same Page, 2015.

Murphy, Tim, and Loriann Oberlin. *Overcoming Passive-Aggression: How to Stop Hidden Anger from Spoiling Your Relationships, Career, and Happiness.* Boston: Da Capo, 2016.

Noll, Douglas E. *De-escalate: How to Calm an Angry Person in 90 Seconds or Less.* New York: Atria Paperback, 2017.

Priolo, Lou. *The Heart of Anger: Practical Help for the Prevention and Cure of Anger in Children.* Sand Springs, OK: Grace & Truth Books, 2015.

Whitehouse, Éliane, and Warwick Pudney. *A Volcano in My Tummy: Helping Children to Handle Anger.* Gabriola Island, BC: New Society, 1996.

Wilde, Jerry. *Hot Stuff to Help Kids Chill Out: The Anger Management Book.* Richmond, IN: LGR, 1997.

Brain Development

Siegel, Daniel J. *Brainstorm: The Power and Purpose of the Teenage Brain.* New York: TarcherPerigee, 2015.

Siegel, Daniel J., and Tina Payne Bryson. *The Whole-Brain Child: 12 Revolutionary Strategies to Nurture Your Child's Developing Mind.* New York: Bantam Books, 2012.

Suskind, Dana. *Thirty Million Words: Building a Child's Brain.* New York: Dutton, 2015.

Communication

Faber, Adele, and Elaine Mazlish. *How to Talk So Kids Will Listen and Listen So Kids Will Talk.* New York: Scribner, 2012.

Connecting with Children

Bailey, Becky A. *I Love You Rituals.* New York: HarperCollins, 2000.

Chapman, Gary D., and Ross Campbell. *The 5 Love Languages of Children: The Secret to Loving Children Effectively.* Chicago: Northfield, 2016.

Chapman, Gary. *The 5 Love Languages of Teenagers: The Secret to Loving Teens Effectively.* Chicago: Northfield, 2016.

Discipline

Siegel, Daniel J., and Tina Payne Bryson. *No-Drama Discipline: The Whole-Brain Way to Calm the Chaos and Nurture Your Child's Developing Mind.* New York: Bantam Books, 2016.

Emotions/Social Awareness

Goff, Sissy, David Thomas, and Melissa Trevathan. *Are My Kids on Track? The 12 Emotional, Social, and Spiritual Milestones Your Child Needs to Reach.* Bloomington, MN: Bethany House, 2017.

Rapee, Ronald M., Ann Wignall, Susan H. Spence, Vanessa Cobham, and Heidi Lyneham. *Helping Your Anxious Child: A Step-by-Step Guide for Parents.* Oakland, CA: New Harbinger, 2008.

Thompson, Curt. *The Soul of Shame: Retelling the Stories We Believe about Ourselves.* Downers Grove, IL: InterVarsity Press, 2015.

Van Dijk, Sheri. *Don't Let Your Emotions Run Your Life for Teens: Dialectical Behavior Therapy Skills for Helping You Manage Mood Swings, Control Angry Outbursts, and Get Along with Others.* Oakland, CA: Instant Help Books, 2011.

Food Allergies

Sicherer, Scott H. *Food Allergies: A Complete Guide for Eating When Your Life Depends on It.* Baltimore: Johns Hopkins University Press, 2017.

Parenting

Cline, Foster, and Jim Fay. *Parenting Teens with Love and Logic: Preparing Adolescents for Responsible Adulthood.* Colorado Springs: Piñon, 2006.

———. *Parenting with Love and Logic: Teaching Children Responsibility.* Colorado Springs: NavPress, 2006.

Eggerichs, Emerson. *Love and Respect in the Family: The Respect Parents Desire, The Love Children Need.* Nashville, TN: Thomas Nelson, 2013.

Feldhahn, Shaunti, and Lisa A. Rice. *For Parents Only: Getting Inside the Head of Your Kid.* Colorado Springs: Multnomah, 2007.

Goyer, Tricia. *Walk It Out: The Radical Result of Living God's Word One Step at a Time.* Colorado Springs: David C Cook, 2017.

Siegel, Daniel J., and Mary Hartzell. *Parenting from the Inside Out: How a Deeper Self-Understanding Can Help You Raise Children Who Thrive.* New York: TarcherPerigee, 2004.

Workbooks

Allender, Dan B. *Healing the Wounded Heart Workbook: The Heartache of Sexual Abuse and the Hope of Transformation.* With Traci Mullins. Grand Rapids, MI: Baker Books, 2016.

Guest, Jennifer. *The CBT Art Activity Book: 100 Illustrated Handouts for Creative Therapeutic Work.* London: Jessica Kingsley, 2015.

Halloran, Janine. *Coping Skills for Kids Workbook: Over 75 Coping Strategies to Help Kids Deal with Stress, Anxiety and Anger.* n.p.: Encourage Play, LLC, 2016.

Lite, Lori. *Angry Octopus Color Me Happy, Color Me Calm: A Self-Help Kid's Coloring Book for Overcoming Anxiety, Anger, Worry, and Stress.* Marietta, GA: Stress Free Kids, 2017.

Shapiro, Lawrence E. *The ADHD Workbook for Kids: Helping Children Gain Self-Confidence, Social Skills, and Self-Control.* Oakland, CA: Instant Help Books, 2010.

Siegel, Daniel J., and Tinay Payne Bryson. *The Whole-Brain Child Workbook: Practical Exercises, Worksheets and Activities to Nurture Developing Minds.* Eau Claire, WI: PESI Publishing & Media, 2015.

Solin, Jennifer J., and Christina L. Kress. *Don't Let Your Emotions Run Your Life for Kids: A DBT-Based Skills Workbook to Help Children Manage Mood Swings, Control Angry Outbursts, and Get Along with Others.* Oakland, CA: Instant Help Books, 2017.

Fiction for Teens Dealing with Foster Care

Jones, Jenny B. *In Between.* A Katie Parker Production 1. Sweet Pea Productions, 2014.

———. *On the Loose.* A Katie Parker Production 2. Sweet Pea Productions, 2014.

———. *The Big Picture.* A Katie Parker Production 3. Sweet Pea Productions, 2014.

Card Games

Chill Skills in a Jar®: Anger Management Tips for Teens. Minneapolis, MN: Free Spirit.

Feelings in a Jar®: A Fun Game for All Ages for Endless Play and Interaction. Minneapolis, MN: Free Spirit.

Mad Dragon: An Anger Control Card Game. Therapy Game HQ.

Temper Tamers in a Jar®: Helping Kids Cool Off and Manage Anger. Minneapolis, MN: Free Spirit.

Think Twice in a Jar®: Think Hard and Think Fun! A Decision-Making Game for All Ages. Minneapolis, MN: Free Spirit.

Books for Preschoolers

Agassi, Martine. *Hands Are Not for Hitting.* Illustrated by Marieka Heinlen. Minneapolis, MN: Free Spirit, 2009.

Dewdney, Anna. *Llama Llama Mad at Mama.* New York: Viking, 2007.

Mayer, Mercer. *I Was So Mad.* New York: Golden Books, 2004.

Verdick, Elizabeth. *Words Are Not for Hurting.* Illustrated by Marieka Heinlen. Minneapolis, MN: Free Spirit, 2004.

Books for Children

Berry, Joy. *Let's Talk about Feeling Angry.* New York: Scholastic, 1995.

Butterfield, Moira. *Everybody Feels Angry!* Illustrated by Holly Sterling. Lake Forest, CA: QEB, 2016.

Cain, Janan. *The Way I Feel.* Seattle, WA: Parenting Press, 2000.

Cook, Julia. *My Mouth Is a Volcano!* Illustrated by Carrie Hartman. Chattanooga, TN: National Center for Youth Issues, 2005.

———. *Wilma Jean the Worry Machine.* Illustrated by Anita DuFalla. Chattanooga, TN: National Center for Youth Issues, 2012.

Curtis, Jamie Lee. *Today I Feel Silly: And Other Moods That Make My Day.* Illustrated by Laura Cornell. New York: Joanna Cotler Books, 1998.

Fox, Laura. *I Am So Angry, I Could Scream: Helping Children Deal with Anger.* Illustrated by Chris Sabatino. Far Hills, NJ: New Horizon, 2000.

Graves, Sue. *Tiger Has a Tantrum: A Book about Feeling Angry.* Illustrated by Trevor Dunton. New York: Franklin Watts, 2016.

Huebner, Dawn. *What to Do When You Worry Too Much: A Kid's Guide to Overcoming Anxiety.* Illustrated by Bonnie Matthews. Washington, DC: Magination, 2006.

———. *What to Do When Your Temper Flares: A Kid's Guide to Overcoming Problems with Anger.* Illustrated by Bonnie Matthews. Washington, DC: Magination, 2007.

Lite, Lori. *Angry Octopus: A Relaxation Story.* Illustrated by Max Stasuyk. Marietta, GA: Stress Free Kids, 2011.

Lucado, Max. *You Are Special.* Illustrated by Sergio Martinez. Wheaton, IL: Crossway, 2002.

McCloud, Carol. *Have You Filled a Bucket Today? A Guide to Daily Happiness for Kids.* Illustrated by David Messing. Brighton, MI: Bucket Fillers, 2016.

McGuire, Andy. *Remy the Rhino Learns Patience.* Eugene, OR: Harvest House, 2010.

Meiners, Cheri J. *Cool Down and Work through Anger.* Minneapolis, MN: Free Spirit, 2017.

Mundy, Michaelene. *Mad Isn't Bad: A Child's Book about Anger.* Illustrated by R. W. Alley. St. Meinrad, IN: Abbey Press, 1999.

Smith, Bryan. *What Were You Thinking? A Story about Learning to Control Your Impulses.* Illustrated by Lisa M. Griffin. Boys Town, NE: Boys Town, 2016.

Spelman, Cornelia Maude. *When I Feel Angry.* Illustrated by Nancy Cote. Morton Grove, IL: Albert Whitman, 2000.

Websites

Aha! Parenting—www.ahaparenting.com

Attention Deficit Disorder Association (ADDA)—www.add.org

Child Mind Institute—www.childmind.org

Coping Skills for Kids—www.copingskillsforkids.com

Empowered to Connect—www.empoweredtoconnect.org

International Dyslexia Association—https://dyslexiaida.org

Kids with Food Allergies—https://community.kidswithfoodallergies.org

Learning Disabilities Association of America—www.ldaamerica.org

The National Child Traumatic Stress Network—www.nctsn.org

STAR Institute for Sensory Processing Disorder—www.spdstar.org

Young Living Essential Oils—www.myyl.com/triciagoyer

NOTES

Chapter 1

1. "PTSD in Children and Teens," PTSD: National Center for PTSD, US Department of Veterans Affairs, last updated August 13, 2015, www.ptsd .va.gov/public/family/ptsd-children-adolescents.asp.

Chapter 2

1. Cristine Bolley, Facebook message to author, October 18, 2017.

2. Deanna Allen, Facebook message to author, October 18, 2017.

3. Heather Berryhill, Facebook message to author, October 18, 2017.

4. Janet McHenry, Facebook message to author, October 18, 2017.

5. Daniel J. Siegel, *Mindsight: The New Science of Personal Transformation* (New York: Bantam Books, 2011), 6.

6. "Anger and Trauma," Elements Behavioral Health, September 15, 2010, www.elementsbehavioralhealth.com/trauma-ptsd/anger-and-trauma/.

7. "Staying Close to Your Tween Daughter," Aha! Parenting, accessed February 7, 2018, www.ahaparenting.com/Ages-stages/tweens/staying-close.

Chapter 3

1. "Is My Child's Anger Normal?" Child Mind Institute, accessed February 7, 2018, www.childmind.org/article/is-my-childs-anger-normal/.

2. "ADHD Symptoms," Child Development Institute, accessed April 20, 2018, https://childdevelopmentinfo.com/add-adhd/adhd-symptoms/.

3. "Is My Child's Anger Normal?"

4. "Pediatric Anxiety," Children's National Health System, accessed February 7, 2018, www.childrensnational.org/choose-childrens/conditions-and -treatments/mental-health-behavioral-disorders/anxiety.

5. "Is My Child's Anger Normal?"

6. Melvyn R. Werbach, "Nutritional Influences on Aggressive Behavior," *Journal of Orthomolecular Medicine* 7, no. 1 (1995), www.orthomolecular.org/library /articles/webach.shtml.

7. Werbach, "Nutritional Influences on Aggressive Behavior."

8. Cheryl Schafer, "Anger and Aggressive Behavior in Teens," LiveStrong.com, May 16, 2015, www.livestrong.com/article/119628-anger-aggressive-behavior -teens/.

9. Mary Brophy Marcus, "New Sleep Guidelines for Babies, Kids and Teens," CBS News, June 13, 2016, www.cbsnews.com/news/new-sleep-guidelines-for -babies-kids-and-teens/.

10. "Staying Close to Your Tween Daughter," Aha! Parenting, accessed February 7, 2018, www.ahaparenting.com/Ages-stages/tweens/staying-close.

Chapter 4

1. Brené Brown, *The Gifts of Imperfection: Let Go of Who You Think You're Supposed to Be and Embrace Who You Are* (Center City, MN: Hazelden, 2010), 61.

2. Henri J. M. Nouwen, *Sabbatical Journey: The Diary of His Final Year* (New York: Crossroad, 1998), 61.

Chapter 5

1. Robert Fulghum, as quoted in Bonita Jean Zimmer, *Reflections for Tending the Sacred Garden: Embracing the Art of Slowing Down* (Lincoln, NE: iUniverse, 2003), 182.

2. Brené Brown, "Be the Adult You Want Your Children to Be," interview by Jennifer Kogan, *Washington Post*, October 5, 2012, www.washingtonpost .com/blogs/on-parenting/post/brene-brown-be-the-adult-you-want-your -children-to-be/2012/10/04/b5bdbd9c-0ca6-11e2-a310-2363842b7057 _blog.html?utm_term=.116f9688107c.

3. Jim Fay and Charles Fay, *Love and Logic Magic for Early Childhood: Practical Parenting from Birth to Six Years* (Golden, CO: Love and Logic, 2000), 19.

Chapter 6

1. "Staying Connected with Your Child," Aha! Parenting, accessed February 7, 2018, www.ahaparenting.com/parenting-tools/connection/staying-connected.

2. Amy Banks, "Humans Are Hardwired for Connection? Neurobiology 101 for Parents, Educators, Practitioners and the General Public," interview, Wellesley Centers for Women, September 15, 2010, www.wcwonline.org/2010 /humans-are-hardwired-for-connection-neurobiology-101-for-parents -educators-practitioners-and-the-general-public.

3. Amy Lively, *How to Love Your Neighbor without Being Weird* (Bloomington, MN: Bethany House), 31–32.

4. *The Sound of Music*, directed by Robert Wise (Robert Wise Productions, 1965).

5. Gary Chapman, *The 5 Love Languages of Teenagers: The Secret to Loving Teens Effectively* (Chicago: Northfield, 2010), 153.

6. Gary Chapman's original book on love languages, *The 5 Love Languages: The Secret to Love That Lasts* (Chicago: Northfield, 2015), identifies these as the primary ways to communicate love to someone. If you are unfamiliar with his book, I highly recommend it.

Chapter 7

1. Anita Bohensky, *Anger Management Workbook for Kids and Teens* (New York: Growth, 2003), 12.

2. Bohensky, *Anger Management Workbook*, 12.

3. Daniel Siegel, "Dr. Daniel Siegel Presenting a Hand Model of the Brain," YouTube, February 29, 2012, www.youtube.com/watch?v=gm9CIJ74Oxw.

4. Daniel Siegel, *Mindsight: The New Science of Personal Transformation* (New York: Bantam Books, 2011), 14–22.

5. "Anger—How It Affects People," Better Health Channel, Department of Health & Human Services, January 2014, www.betterhealth.vic.gov.au/health /healthyliving/anger-how-it-affects-people.

6. Bohensky, *Anger Management Workbook*, 12.

7. "Frontal Lobe," Healthline, March 2, 2015, www.healthline.com/human-body -maps/frontal-lobe/.

8. "Understanding the Teen Brain," Health Encyclopedia, University of Rochester Medical Center, accessed February 15, 2018, www.urmc.rochester.edu /encyclopedia/content.aspx?ContentTypeID=1&ContentID=3051.

9. "Catch It, Check It, Change It," BBC Headroom Wellbeing Guide, accessed February 7, 2018, http://downloads.bbc.co.uk/headroom/cbt/catch_it.pdf.

Chapter 8

1. Aaron Karmin, "What Happens to Your Thoughts and Behaviors When You're Angry?," Psych Central, accessed February 7, 2018, https://blogs .psychcentral.com/anger/2016/05/what-happens-to-your-thoughts-and -behaviors-when-youre-angry/.

2. Douglas E. Noll, *De-escalate: How to Calm an Angry Person in 90 Seconds or Less* (New York: Atria Paperback, 2017), 10.

3. Noll, *De-escalate*, 10.

4. Noll, *De-escalate*, 15–16.

5. Noll, *De-escalate*, 18.

6. Jerry Wilde, *Hot Stuff to Help Kids Chill Out: The Anger Management Book* (Richmond, IN: LGR, 1997), 45–46.

Chapter 9

1. Joseph Castro, "How a Mother's Love Changes a Child's Brain," Live Science, January 30, 2012, www.livescience.com/18196-maternal-support-child-brain .html.

2. Karen DeBord, "Brain Development," Pregnacy & Baby, SheKnows, accessed April 26, 2018, http://pregnancyandbaby.com/baby/articles/939213/brain -development.

3. "Early Brain Development," Ready to Succeed, University of California, accessed February 7, 2018, http://ucanr.edu/sites/ReadytoSucceed/Articles_of _Interest/Early_Brain_Development/.

4. Dana Suskind, *Thirty Million Words: Building a Child's Brain* (New York: Dutton, 2015), 56.

5. Janine Watson, "Helping Children with Eating" (lecture, The CALL of Saline County Adoptive and Foster Parent Retreat, n.p., November 3, 2017).

6. Daniel J. Siegel and Tina Payne Bryson, *The Whole-Brain Child: 12 Revolutionary Strategies to Nurture Your Child's Developing Mind* (New York: Bantam Books, 2012), 16.

7. Suskind, *Thirty Million Words*, 115.

8. Suskind, *Thirty Million Words*, 160.

9. Siegel and Bryson, *The Whole-Brain Child*, xi.

Chapter 10

1. Tom Burns, "25 Things I Think Every Dad Should Teach His Kids," Huffington Post, June 9, 2014, www.huffingtonpost.com/2013/02/20/advice-from-dads_n_2725140.html.

2. Foster Cline and Jim Fay, *Parenting without the Power Struggles* (Colorado Springs: NavPress, 2013), chap. 3, Kindle.

3. James Lehman, "Angry Child? Fix the Behavior, Not the Feelings," Empowering Parents, accessed February 14, 2018, www.empoweringparents.com/article/angry-child-fix-the-behavior-not-the-feelings/.

4. "Staying Close to Your Tween Daughter," Aha! Parenting, accessed February 7, 2018, www.ahaparenting.com/Ages-stages/tweens/staying-close.

Chapter 11

1. Foster Cline and Jim Fay, *Parenting Teens with Love and Logic: Preparing Adolescents for Responsible Adulthood* (Colorado Springs: Piñon, 2006), 17.

2. Gary Chapman, *The 5 Love Languages of Teenagers: The Secret to Loving Teens Effectively* (Chicago: Northfield, 2016), 182.

3. William Shakespeare, *The Taming of the Shrew*, ed. H. J. Oliver (Oxford: Oxford University Press, 1982), 198.

4. D. Ross Campbell, *How to Really Love Your Angry Child*, with Rob Suggs (Colorado Springs: Life Journey, 2003), 79.

5. Campbell, *How to Really Love Your Angry Child*, 80.

6. Lynn Weiss, quoted in Janis Leibs Dworkis, "Behind the Mask of Teenage Anger," *Scouting*, September 2002, 30.

7. Chapman, *The 5 Love Languages of Teenagers*, 190.

8. Chapman, *The 5 Love Languages of Teenagers*, 180.

Chapter 12

1. Russell A. Barkley, *Taking Charge of ADHD: The Complete, Authoritative Guide for Parents* (New York: Guilford, 2013), 5.

2. Daniel J. Siegel and Tina Payne Bryson, *The Whole-Brain Child: 12 Revolutionary Strategies to Nurture Your Child's Developing Mind* (New York: Bantam Books, 2012), xii.

3. Lesley Stoll, Facebook message to author, October 18, 2017.

4. Douglas E. Noll, *De-escalate: How to Calm an Angry Person in 90 Seconds or Less* (New York: Atria Paperback, 2017), 38.

5. Curt Thompson, *The Soul of Shame: Retelling the Stories We Believe about Ourselves* (Downers Grove, IL: InterVarsity Press, 2015), 29.

6. Kathryn Patricelli, "Effects of Abuse," December 15, 2005, MentalHelp.net, www.mentalhelp.net/articles/effects-of-abuse/.

7. Yyuvone Heidelberger, "The Costume of Many Foster Children," The CALL, accessed January 31, 2018, http://us6.campaign-archive.com/?e=370ffea522&u=a3fa7f07a663fe6ce666f2381&id=7f3bce16c9.

Conclusion

1. J. Scott Duvall, *Revelation*, Teach the Text Commentary Series (Grand Rapids, MI: Baker Books, 2017), 54.

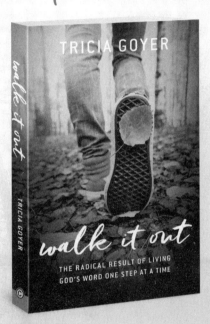